The Guide to Basic
COVER LETTER
WRITING

PUBLIC LIBRARY
ASSOCIATION
A division of the American Library Association

The Public Library Association and the Editors of VGM Career Books

The Guide to Basic
COVER LETTER
WRITING

SECOND EDITION

VGM Career Books

Chicago   New York   San Francisco   Lisbon   London   Madrid   Mexico City
Milan   New Delhi   San Juan   Seoul   Singapore   Sydney   Toronto

Library of Congress Cataloging-in-Publication Data is available through the Library of Congress.

1 2 3 4 5 6 7 8 9 0   QPD/QPD   2 1 0 9 8 7 6 5 4 3

ISBN 0-07-140590-9

McGraw-Hill books are available at special quantity discounts to use as premiums and sales promotions, or for use in corporate training programs. For more information, please write to the Director of Special Sales, Professional Publishing, McGraw-Hill, Two Penn Plaza, New York, NY 10121-2298. Or contact your local bookstore.

This book is printed on acid-free paper.

Contents

Foreword   *vii*

Acknowledgments   *ix*

Introduction   *xi*

Part I

General Information About Cover Letters   *1*

  The Purpose of the Cover Letter   *1*

  Producing the Cover Letter   *2*

  Personalize Your Presentation   *3*

  Employers Need to Know: What Can You Do for Me?   *4*

  Part of a Targeted Job Search   *5*

Part II

Essential Guidelines for Writing Cover Letters   *7*

  The Basics of Writing a Cover Letter   *7*

  Overall Format   *8*

  General Procedure   *9*

  Before You Begin Writing: Research, Research, Research!   *10*

  Reinforce Key Points of Your Resume   *11*

  Highlight Applicable Skills and Achievements   *11*

  General Grammar Rules for Cover Letters   *12*

  Cover Letter Content: Primary Points   *12*

  Formatting Your Letter   *13*

  Professional Printing and Appearance   *14*

Part III

Advice from the Experts   *15*

Part IV

Cover Letter Examples for Various Positions   29
    Entry-Level, Semi-Skilled, or General Employment   29
    Skilled Tradesperson   38
    Professional/Management   57
    Special Situations   79
    Additional Cover Letter Fragments   90
    Follow-Up Letters   104
    Reference and Salary History Sheets   108

Part V

Printing and Distributing Your Cover Letter and Resume   113
    Where to Use   113
    Tips on Mailing and Follow-Up   115
    Motivation Is Essential   116

Part VI

The Interview   119

Appendix A: Further Reading   121

Appendix B: Selected Organizations of Interest   125

Appendix C: Action Words   127

Foreword

When you are starting a job search, where is the first place you should look? Is it the newspaper's want ad section? A career counselor at your school or a certified career coach? Employers' websites? The placement office at your school? An employment agency? All of these sources have advantages, but there's another place you should look first.

The place to begin your job search is your local public library. Public libraries are your one-stop source for information on how to launch a successful job search. You can find books on resume writing or career selection, and you may even find videos on how to interview successfully. Many libraries also have computers that patrons may use for Internet searches or other functions.

The public library can be your partner throughout your career. The library can provide current economic information and ideas for improving your company's products or services, or help in launching your own business. Your public librarian can be one of your greatest assets as you pursue your professional life.

For all these reasons, the Public Library Association is proud to work with VGM Career Books on this necessary reference.

George Needham
Former Executive Director
Public Library Association

Acknowledgments

The Job and Career Information Services Committee, Adult Lifelong Learning Section, Public Library Association, a division of the American Library Association, assisted in the preparation of the first edition of the *Guide to Basic Cover Letter Writing*. Members of the committee who contributed materials for the original version of this book, with their affiliations at the time of original publication, were:

Steve Oserman (cochair), Skokie (Illinois) Public Library; Ruth Schwab (cochair), Ossining (New York) Public Library; Marianne Fairfield, Cuyahoga County (Ohio) Public Library; Vera Green, Carnegie Library of Pittsburgh (Pennsylvania); Margaret Herman, El Paso (Texas) Public Library; Joan Jackson, San Francisco (California) Public Library; Martin Jaffe, Cuyahoga County (Ohio) Public Library, Maple Heights Regional Branch; Mark Leggett, Indianapolis-Marion County (Indiana) Public Library; James Lyons, St. Louis (Missouri) Public Library; Theodore Mason, East Chicago (Indiana) Public Library, Erlinda Regner, Harold Washington Library (Chicago, Illinois); Frances Roehm, Bloomington (Illinois) Public Library; Sue Schlaf, Schaumburg Township (Illinois) District Library.

A special acknowledgment must go to Steven Provenzano who contributed greatly to the first edition of this book. He is the president of a successful professional resume service. As such, he has written more than 3,000 resumes and cover letters. He also consults with clients on resume and cover letter preparation, as well as working as a writer and designer.

The second edition of the *Guide to Basic Cover Letter Writing* was undertaken by the Editors of VGM Career Books in tandem with the Public Library Association. The editors also wish to thank Mark Rowh for his valuable assistance with this second edition.

Introduction

This book is designed to work in tandem with the *Guide to Basic Resume Writing* and the *Guide to Internet Job Searching*, all of which are essential resources for finding and landing your ideal job. These three books cover all the bases, from gathering information to writing and designing your cover letter and resume and from researching jobs in a variety of fields to applying online.

Because a resume alone cannot highlight a person's individual style the way a cover letter can, the cover letter is an essential part of the job search. Together, an effective cover letter and resume can greatly increase your chances of getting a good job in less time, and can even result in higher pay and better working conditions.

The cover letter allows the job applicant to discuss the needs of the employer, rather than just the applicant's own need for a position. It gives the job applicant a forum for personalizing each application, while targeting specific companies through research and a customized approach.

An investment of time and effort to write a targeted, high-quality cover letter is an investment in your future. Take the time to read through the cover letter examples in this book. There may be sentences, wordings, or phrases that apply to your situation, and you can use these to script your own cover letter to market your abilities and to tell employers why you want to work specifically for them.

In addition, inside this book, you'll find valuable information and expert advice from a variety of career counselors and coaches offering you the latest tips and techniques for producing effective cover letters.

If this book is your own personal copy, you can underline sentences and information that you feel would be most helpful, and return to those sections when writing your own cover letter. It is this extra effort and determination that employers are looking for, and it can help you produce a winning cover letter and expand your employment opportunities for a brighter future.

We wish you the best of luck in your job search!

General Information About Cover Letters

Typically, when you begin the job search and application process, the first thing you do is make sure you have an up-to-date, concise and impressive resume. For detailed information and instructions on crafting an outstanding resume, you should turn to one of the companion guides to this book, the *Guide to Basic Resume Writing*. After you have your polished and professional resume in hand and you've located and researched the job for which you'll be applying, you need to write a targeted cover letter that speaks to the company's needs and sells yourself as the ideal candidate for the job.

THE PURPOSE OF THE COVER LETTER

Cover letters accompany your resume and serve the purpose of highlighting the specific skills you possess that will be of interest to the prospective employer. While there may be instances where you deliver your resume in person, you will usually send it through the mail or online. Resumes sent through the mail always need an accompanying letter that briefly introduces you and your resume. The purpose of the cover letter is to compel a potential employer to read your resume, just as the purpose of the resume is to convince that same potential employer to call you for an interview. It is used primarily to:

- Introduce yourself and the resume that follows.

- Show employers that you understand their company/organization, and have at least a basic knowledge of their products, services, markets, and/or employment needs.

- Tell employers why and how your qualifications can help their specific business or organization (for example: increase sales, reduce costs, or improve efficiency).

- Expand on key points listed in an advertisement or job description. You can use wording directly from the advertisement for this purpose.

- Request an interview to discuss matters that could be of mutual interest, or tell the reader that you'll call him or her to discuss the position and arrange a meeting.

PRODUCING THE COVER LETTER

Like your resume, your cover letter should be clean, neat, and direct. A cover letter usually includes the following information:

1. Your name and address (unless it already appears on your personal letterhead) and your phone number(s); see item 7.

2. The date.

3. The name and address of the person and company to whom you are sending your resume.

4. The salutation ("Dear Mr." or "Dear Ms." followed by the person's last name, or "To Whom It May Concern" if you are answering a blind ad).

5. An opening paragraph explaining why you are writing (for example, in response to an ad, as a follow-up to a previous meeting, at the suggestion of a mutual acquaintance) and indicating that you are interested in whatever job is being offered.

6. One or more paragraphs that tell why you want to work for the company and what qualifications and experiences you can bring to the position. This is a good place to mention some detail about that particular company that makes you want to work for them; this shows that you have done some research before applying.

7. A final paragraph that closes the letter and invites the reviewer to contact you for an interview. This can be a good place to tell the potential employer which method would be best to use when contacting you. Be sure to give the correct phone number and a good time to reach you, if that is important. You may mention here that your references are available upon request.

8. The closing ("Sincerely" or "Yours truly") followed by your signature in a dark ink, with your name typed under it.

Your cover letter should include all of this information and be no longer than one page in length. The language used should be polite, businesslike, and to the point. Don't attempt to tell your life story in the cover letter; a long and cluttered letter will serve only to annoy the reader. Remember that you need to mention only a few of your accomplishments and skills in the cover letter. The rest of your information is available in your resume. If your cover letter is a success, your prospective employer will read your resume and will review all pertinent information.

After you have written your cover letter, proofread it as thoroughly as you did your resume. Again, spelling or punctuation errors are a sure sign of carelessness, and you don't want that to be a part of your first impression on a prospective employer. This is no time to trust your spell-check function. Even after going through a spelling and grammar check, your cover letter should be carefully proofread by at least one other person.

Print the cover letter on the same quality bond paper you used for your resume. Remember to sign it, using a good pen with black ink. Handle the letter and resume carefully to avoid smudging or wrinkling, and mail them together in an appropriately sized envelope. Many stores sell matching envelopes to coordinate with your choice of bond paper.

Keep an accurate record of all resumes you send out and the results of each mailing. This record can be kept on your computer, in a calendar or notebook, or on file cards. Knowing when a resume is likely to have been received will keep you on track as you make follow-up phone calls.

About a week after mailing resumes and cover letters to potential employers, contact them by telephone. Confirm that your resume arrived and ask whether an interview might be possible. Be sure to record the name of the person you spoke to and any other information you gleaned from the conversation. It is wise to treat the person answering the phone with a great deal of respect; sometimes the assistant or receptionist has the ear of the person doing the hiring.

PERSONALIZE YOUR PRESENTATION

Cover letters should always be individualized because they are always written to specific individuals and companies. Never use a form letter for your cover letter or copy it as you would a resume. Each cover letter should be unique, and as personal and lively as possible. (Of course, once you have written and rewritten your first cover letter until you are satisfied with it, you can certainly use similar wording in subsequent letters. You may want to save a template on your computer for future reference.) Keep a hard copy of each cover letter so that you know exactly what you wrote in each one. Remember that every letter is unique and depends on your particular circumstances and the job for which you are applying.

A resume alone cannot highlight your personal skills the way a cover letter can. A well-written cover letter allows you to discuss the needs of the potential employer rather than your own needs, and give several key reasons why you should be interviewed for the position. You must clearly demonstrate how you would apply your skills, training, and experience to help an organization achieve its goals better than anyone else.

The letter helps convey those personal qualities and desires that may not belong in your resume, such as self-motivation, desire to travel or relocate, or excellent record of attendance. A good letter sets you apart from applicants who submit only resumes or applications. It gives you a way to personalize each resume you send, while targeting companies through research and a customized approach. Your cover letter must focus the reader on your particular skills and provide good reasons to continue reading the resume and/or application that follows.

EMPLOYERS NEED TO KNOW: WHAT CAN YOU DO FOR ME?

Always keep in mind that the employers want to see what you can do for them. After all, this is why employers are reading your letter and resume in the first place. Too many people writing cover letters discuss only what they want in a position. Of course, what you want in a job—and why you're sending information about yourself—is very important. But you must then tell employers how your skills can help them achieve their goals. In other words, the content of your cover letter needs to be a combination of what you want in a job and how the employers will benefit by hiring you.

Here's a tip that can help save time and make it easy to personalize your cover letters: After reading the instructions in this book and checking the cover letter examples, write a cover letter that emphasizes the primary skills and abilities you would like to use most on the job and that you feel are valuable to most of the employers who'll be reading your letter. To customize your letter so that it can be sent to more than one employer, first address each copy to the appropriate hiring authority (call each company if possible to find this, or simply use the name/designation in the advertisement or job listing). Then rewrite the first paragraph of the cover letter and mention the company and aspects of the position about which you're most interested.

PART OF A TARGETED JOB SEARCH

The current job market may be the most competitive in recent history. In many cases, there are simply too many applicants for too few well-paying skilled or semiskilled positions. This is why many employers place such a strong emphasis on cover letters and resumes as their first impression of an applicant's skills, abilities, and overall experience.

This is also why employers appreciate a targeted job search: Employers need to feel that you took the time and effort to target their company specifically, and that you take a special interest in working for them. This method of finding job interviews is usually much more effective than the shotgun approach of sending out impersonal resumes or applications to hundreds of companies. See the bibliography at the end of this book for materials on job hunting, correctly using resumes and cover letters, and interviewing to expand your knowledge of effective job-hunting strategies.

Most letters and resumes get only a few seconds of attention from busy human resources staff or hiring managers, and you must get your point across promptly and clearly. Your cover letter must have clarity and impact, and must be grammatically correct and easy for readers to absorb quickly at a glance. That's why most samples in this book are short and to the point.

Whatever type of cover letter you produce, make sure you proofread it very carefully. Show it to family, friends, and business associates and get their opinions. Nothing turns off an employer more than a cover letter or resume with mistakes such as bad spelling, poor grammar, or hard-to-read type. These areas are all covered later.

Essential Guidelines
for Writing Cover Letters

THE BASICS OF WRITING A COVER LETTER

Your cover letter can follow any of the general formats shown in this book, but most important, it must always include the following elements:

1. Who you are: Your name, address, telephone number with area code, and E-mail address, if available.

2. Why you're sending the employer the cover letter. State clearly your intention in sending the letter and the actual title of the job you're seeking (or the general type of work you're looking for), such as Warehouse Operations, Shipping/Receiving, Accounting or Book-keeping, or Sales/Marketing). Use the advertisement or job description whenever possible to help write this portion. If that's unavailable, use a more general approach, such as, "I am seeking a position in which I may better utilize my experience in . . ."

3. A short summary of major accomplishments and achievements at various companies or nonprofit organizations, when appropriate, or an outline of your most important training and education. List key skills, abilities, or training that applies to the position at hand, such as "experienced in the setup of warehouse fixtures," or "skilled in inventory control and stocking on computer systems," or "have a strong aptitude for figures and utilize 10-key calculators," or "have

successful experience in new business development and account management."

4. A short but detailed review or sample of what you know about the company or industry: its products, customers, markets, and way of doing business. Mention that you want to work specifically for that company.

5. Whether you are willing to travel or relocate, if this is a requirement of the position, as in outside sales or driving. You may omit this if it is not requested, or if you are not willing to travel or relocate.

6. Other specifics about yourself or the job. If someone at the company suggested you send your application, mention that person's name. If the posting asks you to include salary requirements, and not salary history, give them a desired salary range and avoid a specific number. For example, you might write "$12-15 per hour, negotiable." You may include this in a letter; however, if both salary requirements and salary history are requested, include them on a separate salary history sheet, and end the page by writing, "Salary requirements are open to negotiation."

7. Thank readers for their time and consideration; let them know that you look forward to a response.

OVERALL FORMAT

Several formats for cover letters are presented in this book, but most consist of an introductory paragraph, the body of the text, and a closing. All of the examples have plenty of white space (space between paragraphs and before and after the text). This makes them easier to read and pleasing to the eye.

Some examples contain bulleted points that help draw the eye and the reader's attention. Consider this format if you have short, key accomplishments or some highly important or successful experience. Simply highlight the information by placing an asterisk, dash, circle, or box before the sentence, or by using a bold font.

You can easily change these bullet points to target specific jobs and develop those aspects of your background you feel are most important to any certain job. In this example, the paragraph is followed with bulleted items:

I am exploring opportunities as a general office assistant with your company because I'm interested in a position that offers the potential for greater challenge and career growth.

My most recent position as an administrative assistant for a large trade book publisher required extensive customer relations, as well as creating spreadsheets, databases, and presentations for a group of five editors. Because of this experience, I can now offer your company:

- Proficiency in Microsoft Word, Excel, and Access, as well as a strong aptitude for learning other computer software.
- Experience in operating a 10-line switchboard while taking messages and scheduling appointments.
- A proven ability to handle customer problems and a wide range of duties in a tactful, professional manner.

I would welcome the opportunity to speak with you personally to discuss how my background can benefit your company. I am willing to relocate for the right opportunity and can provide excellent references at your request.

Thank you for your time and consideration. I look forward to hearing from you soon.

Sincerely,

Wilma Jones
enclosure

In this example, notice how the writer's key skills and abilities stand out from the rest of the letter. You may also notice how the eye is quickly drawn to the bulleted material.

GENERAL PROCEDURE

The general procedure for producing and sending your cover letters is as follows:

1. Always send a cover letter with your resume and personalize it by researching the company. Exceptions can be made for blind box ads.

Include a letter addressed to "Dear Hiring Authority" or "Dear Prospective Employer."

2. Address your letters to an individual whenever possible. If you don't have a name, call the company and get the exact spelling of the hiring authority's name and the person's job title. If that's not available, send it to the personnel manager, human resources representative, or corporate recruiter, with his or her name if possible.

3. If you make your letters brief and to the point, they will stand a much better chance of getting read. Some employers skip over very long letters, so keep your letter down to three to five short paragraphs to increase its readability.

4. Letters should always be produced using a word-processing program like Microsoft Word using an attractive, professional font. Be sure to use the same paper color for both resumes and letters. White, cream, or gray are the most professional-looking paper choices, but if you're in an especially creative field, you may be able to design your own letterhead paper with impressive results. However, be wary of doing this in more conservative fields.

5. Proofread your letter as closely as your resume. Proofread once for content, then once for grammar and typing mistakes. Then read it backwards, and have someone else read it, too.

BEFORE YOU BEGIN WRITING: RESEARCH, RESEARCH, RESEARCH!

As mentioned earlier, employers want to know that you've taken the time to review their hiring needs before sending an application, resume, or cover letter. This is all part of your targeted job search. Keep in mind that if you don't have the time or means to conduct a targeted search, you should still write a letter that emphasizes those skills and abilities that could be utilized by most companies to which you apply.

To begin your research, first review the job description or advertisement, if any. You may also find a company's annual or quarterly report in the library, or call the company and ask the receptionist about the company's products, services, overall size, and markets. Most companies are happy to tell you all about their product lines and ranking in the industry. You can also request or review any brochures or other information on the company. There are several books in the library on publicly held companies, including service or manufacturer directories, produced on a statewide basis. Again, check the bibliography at the end of this book for more information.

Whenever possible, try to get:

1. The hiring authority's precise name and job title.

2. The correct spelling of the company or organization's name.

3. The correct address, including suite number, if any, and ZIP code.

4. The organization's website, if available.

REINFORCE KEY POINTS OF YOUR RESUME

Your resume is a great place to look for words to include in your cover letter. Pull out the most relevant points of your experience and reword them using "I" and "We" for a more personal touch. (If you don't yet have a resume, see the companion volume to this book, the *Guide to Basic Resume Writing*.) Also, check the bibliography at the back of this book for a listing of resume books filled with examples and resume-writing techniques.

If you don't have a resume, take a moment to jot down your most important skills, training, and abilities, whether or not you've done them on the job. Refer to this list when writing your cover letter and insert those items most important to specific positions, perhaps as bulleted points.

HIGHLIGHT APPLICABLE SKILLS AND ACHIEVEMENTS

Once you have an idea about the requirements of the position and the needs of the company, make a list of those qualifications and achievements you believe would be most applicable and valuable to the potential employer. Get a blank piece of paper and start listing items that most apply to the needs of the company(s):

1. Skills learned on the job. Even if you haven't worked at a certain task for several years, list your most applicable skills if you still believe you're qualified and can use them in a new position.

2. Subjects learned in school or college (or in training seminars), but only if you think they are current or important to the position you're seeking.

3. Key accomplishments at previous positions and notable contributions to your previous employers. Perhaps you increased sales (by what percentage?), reduced waste, lowered the cost of production, or raised customer satisfaction.

4. Several of your key personal attributes: Are you self-motivated, energetic, a strong communicator, consistently on-time to work, well-organized, and reliable?

Not all of these points belong in every cover letter. Use those items most relevant to the position. These will change with every letter you write and for every company you approach. When writing a generic cover letter, you can use most or all of these points to help sell your overall qualifications.

GENERAL GRAMMAR RULES FOR COVER LETTERS

As mentioned earlier, your cover letter must be completely free of errors in grammar and spelling. That's because it is the reader's first impression of who you are, what you can do, and your level of professionalism. Always use clear, concise language and avoid repeating words. Avoid beginning more than one sentence with the same word, and try to use business terms that might actually be used by the employer. Remember that you're trying to portray yourself as being a match for the new position, rather than simply showing that you were well qualified for your previous jobs.

When listing a state as part of your return address, use the appropriate postal code rather than the entire state name; for example, use IN for Indiana.

Keep your sentences short and to the point. It's hard to digest run-on or rambling sentences with little or no punctuation. Use one sentence for each key thought, then simply begin another sentence with a related thought. The letter must be light and easy to read, yet still have impact and present important information to the reader.

Again, make sure to proofread all your writing carefully before mailing. Have others read it, too. If you find yourself rushing to get something in the mail, take a moment to slow down and make sure you are sending out high-quality information. Your career is in your hands!

COVER LETTER CONTENT: PRIMARY POINTS

Overall, your cover letter should contain only positive aspects of your background and no negatives. Exceptions can be made if you have a specific aspect about your past that must be explained to employers before requesting an interview. For example, you might include reasons for having held several short-term jobs within a one- or two-year period, but only if this happened because of relocation, major company downsizings, layoffs, or your company going out of business, and only if you're otherwise having trouble getting interviews. If you have served time in prison, be sure to see the cover letter example covering that circumstance. Always be sure to highlight the skills you can currently provide; mention but don't dwell on your past.

Never speak badly of your previous employers, either in your letter or during an interview. Instead, try to state that you left your former position because you were looking for new job challenges, better pay, better hours or working conditions, or greater career advancement.

Also avoid listing your salary history or references in your cover letter. These items belong on separate salary history or reference sheets. (For an explanation of this item, see the *Guide to Basic Resume Writing* or similar books.) You may state your most recent wages or salary requirements in your cover letter only if it is requested in an advertisement or by the employer. If you must list salary information, use only ranges: "mid- to upper $40s per year" or "lower $30s per year."

Most important, your materials must read well, with authority and impact. Don't oversell or undersell your qualifications. Be sure to use direct, no-nonsense, easy-to-understand language.

Remember that cover letters and resumes are designed to get your foot in the door for an interview with an employer so you can present your total qualifications. The interview process is where the details of salary should be discussed.

FORMATTING YOUR LETTER

The following cover letter examples are set in a basic font (Times New Roman) that prints at 12 characters per inch (12 cpi). You may prefer other fonts such as Arial or Courier New. The choice is yours, but avoid any fancy choices that may be difficult to read.

The sample letters that follow are designed to give you a basis for your own customized letters. (The names and addresses of those sending these letters have been changed for confidentiality.) You should also write a very general, boilerplate letter to send to blind box or P.O. box ads, which list only a box number and no company name. A letter sent to a blind box or P.O. box can be specific about your skills but does not need to be specific about the employing company or organization.

Simple block-style letters have no indents or tabs. You can center your name and address on the page to give the appearance of personalized stationery. In some cases, an extra space between each letter of the person's name gives the illusion of larger type and helps the name to stand out in the reader's mind.

The use of boldface or italics can help add style and emphasis to your writing but should not be overused. You might want to experiment with the results of using such highlighting. Remember to read these examples carefully and take notes on a separate sheet of paper. Keep track of sentences and words you can use in your own personalized cover letters.

PROFESSIONAL PRINTING AND APPEARANCE

Once the writing is finished, you should print your resumes using a laser printer or good-quality ink-jet printer. You can also have them professionally printed, but this is not a necessity, and some experts argue against this approach because it incurs needless expense. In any case, the end result should present a professional image and demonstrate that you are serious about the job. If you lack the necessary resources, most quick printers and professional resume services will be happy to help you with this, and many can be found in your local yellow pages. Your library or a college career center (or computer lab) may have computers and printers available for this task. If you can store your cover letter and resume electronically, updates and changes are fast and easy. Always keep backup copies of both documents on paper, just in case the electronic version is lost or damaged. Keeping an extra electronic copy on a diskette or second computer is also wise.

Even general letters to blind boxes, online sites, or P.O. boxes can be personalized by modifying the first two or three paragraphs. Using a word-processing program, insert at least the company name and address, and, preferably, any other information that shows you know about the company and how you can help it.

Part III

Advice from the Experts

Although anyone can develop effective cover letters, it can also be helpful to consult those who specialize in the career search process. In this spirit, the following are a number of common cover letter questions posed to career counselors and other experts, and their responses. Some have chosen to answer only one or two questions, while others have weighed in on a number of topics, providing a variety of helpful tips and advice. In considering the advice provided, keep in mind that there is room for different approaches to cover letter development depending on your work and education experiences as well as the career path you are pursuing. In fact, even the experts sometimes disagree about the finer points of writing effective cover letters. This is an indicator that some flexibility in constructing a cover letter is possible and should set you at ease in building your own outstanding letter.

Good luck in your job search!

Where should I go to get help with developing cover letters?

Kathy Woughter, Director, Career Development Center, Alfred University, Alfred, NY: You can certainly find a resume writing business in most cities, and they'll help with cover letters as well. I would recommend that you also try your local colleges and universities. Their career centers may offer workshops that you'd be welcome to attend. They will certainly have handouts they'll give you, and their websites are a gold mine of that type of advice. They may even allow community members to meet with career counselors.

Of course, there are some great websites out there too. Any mega site, such as Monster or HotJobs, will have tutorials on writing cover letters.

Also, you can go to www.jobweb.org or www.careerplanit.org, both of which are geared toward college students and will certainly have great information on writing job search documents.

Liz Ryan, CEO and Founder, WorldWIT, Boulder, CO: Your friends and business colleagues are a great start. There are terrific free E-mail discussion lists (like WorldWIT, at www.worldwit.org) that can also be useful.

How long should a cover letter be?

Karen S. McAndrew, Director, Office of Career Services, Harvey Mudd College, Claremont, CA: A cover letter should be brief—no longer than one page—and should expand on information contained in the resume that is relevant to the company/position to which it is directed. The introductory paragraph should contain referral information, if applicable, and your reason for applying to this particular company.

Patch Schwadron, Resume Deli, New York, NY: The role of the cover letter is to highlight the skills and experience you offer that most specifically relate to the job or company you are approaching. Generally, this can be achieved in one page. The basic format includes three paragraphs. The first paragraph addresses why you are writing and how you learned about the opportunity. The second paragraph focuses on your special qualifications that make you a suitable candidate for this specific opportunity. And the third paragraph serves to close your letter and includes a mention of follow-up.

Christine Earman Harriger, Career Counselor, George Mason University, Fairfax, VA: A cover letter doesn't need to be lengthy to be effective. A good cover letter is typically only three or four paragraphs in length. The first paragraph should begin with how you heard about the position opening. Employers like to keep track of successful marketing methods. The next sentence should make a strong impact on why you would be a good fit for the position. If your work experience is your strength, then include a sentence to help the reader of your resume quickly understand the value of your experience.

The second paragraph is an opportunity to further elaborate on your skills and qualities. Also, incorporate your research of the company or position to show you have closely examined and considered the position. Do not duplicate what is in your resume but instead highlight what makes you a good match for the position.

In the final paragraph ask for an opportunity to meet with them to further discuss your background and experience. Ask for an interview! Clearly explain the best way for the employer to contact you and include your phone number in the text of the paragraph. Be sure to thank readers in advance for their time and consideration.

A cover letter is a great opportunity to match yourself to the position opening. Never skip an opportunity to market yourself!

Susan W. Miller, National Certified Career Counselor, California Career Services, Los Angeles, CA: The cover letter should be one page and have three paragraphs. The first paragraph should talk about how you made the connection with the company, what you know about them, and why you are writing.

The second paragraph should relate your experience and skills to the qualifications needed for the job, drawing clear parallels between the criteria for the job and your background, for example, "As you can see from the enclosed resume . . . " The second paragraph can also include brief references to your best qualities, for example, high energy, self-starter, or creative problem solver.

The third paragraph is the follow-up. Take responsibility for the follow-up, when appropriate, and say that you will be calling to set up a meeting or appointment, for example, "I am interested in discussing how I can be of service to you and (the company name). With this in mind, I will call you next week to schedule a meeting."

How formal should I be in writing a cover letter?

Michael F. Courteau, Career Development Instructor, The Art Institutes International, Minneapolis, MN: A cover letter is a formal document. Its function is to introduce you. Therefore, you want to take the opportunity to make a professional impression. In addition to using good-quality paper, you also want to make sure that your grammar, spelling, and punctuation are sound. Avoid contractions, since they are designed to mimic speech, and make sure that the tone is formal and professional. Avoid slang and humor, and always close the letter by signing your name in addition to typing it.

Lena Bottos, Compensation Consultant, Salary.com, Wellesley, MA: The level of formality in your cover letter depends somewhat on your relationship to the recipient reading the cover letter. If you do not know the person who is receiving your cover letter, you should be formal. This will convey to a potential employer your business etiquette. If you are familiar with the person receiving the cover letter, you should still structure the cover letter formally. You may address the individual less formally, and you may be a little more relaxed in the tone of your letter, but keep in mind that usually more than one person makes a hiring decision. Your cover letter may be attached with your resume and distributed to other people in the organization. Do not use the cover letter to discuss personal issues that you do not want shared with individuals you do not know and who may have hiring authority.

Should I always include a cover letter when submitting a resume?

Dr. Peter A. Manzi, Career and Educational Counselor and Consultant, Rochester, NY: Absolutely. A cover letter is a direct, succinct form of communication that can powerfully state the case for hiring you. Cover letters are like one-line headlines that work to get you an interview. With hundreds of resumes, both e-forms and regular printed versions, received by HR departments, a well-crafted cover letter is the way in. Cover letters convey more of the style or personality of the applicant and, thus, are more personal. They can also be used to explain content found in a resume that might require clarification. Cover letters can include parameters for seeking the job, such as why you are seeking a job with the company or why the job you are applying for is quite different from other jobs on your resume. Your cover letter may also state that your current employer is not aware of your wanting to change jobs, thus establishing the need to maintain confidentiality.

The best case for sending a cover letter is what happens when you don't. Without a cover letter, how would the person receiving or reviewing your resume know what position you are seeking? Even with a specific objective stated in the resume, there may be several positions for which the resume may be relevant. Not sending a cover letter will strike most HR staff as lazy or slipshod. Cover letters, like resumes, should be flawlessly written and follow standard business format or whatever electronic format is favored by a company. Proofreading is essential, as spell and grammar checks often miss errors.

Dr. Joan Baum, Director, Professional Development, Marymount Manhattan College, New York, NY: Yes. A cover letter shows you know how to write a business letter, which is very important for many positions. It also shows that you can write. Such evidence is much more reliable than saying you have good communication skills. Write and show them! Writing is the number-one need today. Writing means not just demonstrating that you can use a spell check and not make grammatical mistakes, but it also shows you can think and order sentences in a paragraph. Writing involves critical thinking and judgment as much as grammatical skill. What you choose to say is in effect your first interview.

Even if the job notice says to use fax or E-mail, you should still include a cover letter. Cover letters, even if brief, are especially good for jobs that seem to be tech-oriented. You say, in effect, "I'm a computer whiz, but I can also be managerial down the line." Try two short paragraphs so that they can see how you relate ideas.

Christine Earman Harriger: It is important to understand that a cover letter is meant to introduce and complement your resume; it helps the reader interpret the resume the way you want it read. Therefore, I think it is important to submit a cover letter with your resume. Frequently, this is the part of the job search process that people omit if they are unprepared or in a hurry. I would recommend always taking the time to best represent yourself and match yourself to the position.

A cover letter should not be a form letter. A good cover letter reflects the research that the job seeker has performed and matches the skills and work experience of the seeker to the position description. Slow down and take the time to make a good match.

James K. Elkins, National Certified Career Counselor, Career Planning Services, Scarborough, ME: A cover letter should always be submitted with a resume unless the employer specifically states that no letter is desired. First of all, if an employer receives only a resume and has more than one position open, there is no indication as to what position interests you. Second, the cover letter gives you the chance to tell an employer why you should be hired.

Tracy Bowens, Resume Deli, New York, NY: You would never call on someone, especially a stranger, without first introducing yourself. However, this is exactly what you're doing if you send your resume to a potential employer without sending a cover letter; the two go hand in hand. The cover letter serves as your introduction. It says, "Hello. This is who I am, why I'm contacting you, what I can do for you, and why it's in your best interest to interview me." Your resume reinforces your cover letter by giving details about your experience.

If you neglect to send a cover letter, you run the risk of the hiring manager reacting the same way a stranger would react if you just started speaking without introducing yourself. At least when you are dealing with someone face-to-face or on the phone, you may have the opportunity to start over before the person slams the door or hangs up on you. You don't have this luxury when sending a resume through the post or by E-mail. To make a good first impression, always send a cover letter with your resume.

Lena Bottos: Yes, a cover letter is always necessary. It acts as a prologue to your resume. It introduces you to the reader, gives you a voice not inherently communicated in a typical resume, and sets the bar for your ability to communicate in a business environment. If you are sending your resume to a friend, you may be inclined, or even told, not to bother with a cover letter. Keep in mind that the resume will then be sent to the appropriate parties and your acquaintance is now speaking on your behalf. Take control of the situation and speak for yourself. Who better than you to adequately describe who you are and what you are looking for?

Remember, if you E-mail your resume, the text of the E-mail is your cover letter. Treat it as such, even if you're "just E-mailing it to a friend." Always assume your E-mail will be forwarded. Don't be cute or too casual. Do, however, make it clear that you are friends with the person you are E-mailing; whomever your friend sends the E-mail to will be more likely to consider your resume.

Evan Burks, Senior Vice President, Comforce Corporation, Woodbury, NY: Yes, you should always include a cover letter. This allows you to personalize your resume even more, because you can make the letter specific to the job for which you're applying. This is also a great opportunity to showcase your writing skills. Be aware, however, that cover letters can also be fraught with land mines. They can get too wordy, too folksy, or too stiff. And they're an additional opportunity, if you're not careful, to commit errors in punctuation or typos. Keep in mind that interviewers are often looking to weed people out, particularly if they've got to wade through a ton of resumes. Many will automatically exclude you from further consideration if there are errors.

Should I use a cover letter (or its equivalent) if submitting a resume electronically?

Liz Ryan: Yes. In this case you will write a brief introductory letter as you send off the link to your resume, or the resume itself by E-mail. Resumes sent via E-mail must be sent in plain text, as there are so many versions of Word and other word-processing applications that you run the risk of sending an unreadable resume otherwise.

Jeffrey Taylor, Resume Deli, New York, NY: With the Internet revolutionizing the job search and application processes, more employers are encouraging job seekers to do everything online. Since sending a resume via E-mail is only a click away, many job seekers feel that cover letters are no longer necessary. But regardless of how you apply, be sure to submit a cover letter.

Think of a cover letter as a way to introduce yourself to the employer. Whereas a resume is an impersonal document describing skills and work history, letters of interest are excellent ways to showcase writing skills and to describe how well you fit the job description.

Remember to send the documents as attachments, unless the job description states otherwise, because the text in a printed E-mail never appears (visually) as professional as a formatted document.

How much should I individualize my cover letters?

James K. Elkins: While each cover letter you write will contain some similar information concerning your background, it is very important to highlight the experiences and accomplishments that relate to the specific position that you are applying for. Your goal in writing this letter is to convince the employer that you are worth interviewing.

Tracy Bowens: Does an ad for a Mercedes look like an ad for a Jeep? No. Ads highlight the product features that will appeal to the target audience. The point is to differentiate the product from the competition and lure potential buyers into taking the next step—test driving the car.

A cover letter performs the same function. It is selling a product, and that product is you. Yes, all cover letters should contain certain information, but within that structure, there is room to let your voice come through. Don't simply restate your resume. Tell the hiring managers why you are the right person for the job. Don't be shy. Flaunt your skills. Show them exactly what makes you different from all the other applicants they are bound to hear from.

Just as ads lure potential buyers, lure the hiring managers into taking that next step—reading your resume or picking up the phone to invite you for an interview. Don't miss this perfect opportunity to differentiate yourself from the competition.

Joyce Picard, Director, Career Counseling Associates, Newton, MA: Many job search candidates question the need for a personalized cover letter. They wish to develop a form letter and shorten this process, particularly if they are sending multiple inquiries for positions. However, this part of the inquiry process needs individualized attention.

As a rule of thumb, the cover letter should add something beyond the resume. In the first paragraph you should include some reference to the company that indicates personal research, for example, "I am aware of your new line of widgets and would like to be associated with such a forward-looking company" or "The growth of your company and its record as a fine work environment are most appealing." In the second paragraph it is important to expand on some accomplishment cited in the resume as it may relate to the targeted position, for example, "The policies manual completed in Project B, cited in my resume, has been distributed and utilized by the company ever since" or "In addition to my skills and experience, which seem to match your needs, I was acknowledged as a fine team leader in completing multiple projects in a timely fashion."

It is true that some cover letters are not read; however, there is enough anecdotal information regarding eye-catching cover letters to make this effort worthwhile. Puffy and impersonal cover letters are quickly identified by screeners and will not serve you well. Three or four paragraphs are sufficient. Each sentence must say something pointed. Edit the cover letter well. Avoid starting too many sentences with the letter "I," particularly if you are targeting a writing-related position such as one in public relations or marketing. Your cover letter will be the first evidence of your writing skills.

David M. Westhart, Director, Career Development Center, Jefferson College of Health Professions, Thomas Jefferson University, Philadelphia, PA: You should personalize your cover letters as much as possible. I always suggest clients have an "A" list of places they'd like to work and a "B" list. Obviously, more effort is put into tailoring the cover letter for the "A" list. Finding specifics about an organization can be done on the company's website or as a search in the local newspaper's website. Networking with alumni from your school who work at an organization is another great way to get information about a company or organization.

Ellie Augur, Career Counselor, ReadyMinds, www.readyminds.com: The cover letter will work on your behalf when you match your skills with the requirements of the job. Following are tips for individualizing a cover letter:

- Cover letters usually contain three paragraphs. The first and last do not need additional editing except for the name of the particular job or something else unique to the position.

- The second paragraph is of most importance. Be sure that you have researched the company and have a good sense of what they are looking for. Take a statement from your resume describing your accomplishments and skills and develop it further:

  - For example, the requirements for the job include training others. You have recently attended a workshop on this topic. On your resume you wrote that you have trained 10 people. In your cover letter you might write, "Recently I attended a three-day seminar on training. I returned to work to find that the person doing the training at the next level was out sick. I was asked to do the training. My manager complimented me on the job I'd done and asked me to continue with the weekly training sessions."

Evan Burks: It should be individualized for each position. Nothing will fly into an employer's trash can faster than a "form" letter in which you've basically only changed the name of the company.

Susan W. Miller: The cover letter should be individualized, and it is often a good idea to address each qualification the employer is looking for and how your experience and background meet the qualifications for the job. For example, "Your job spec indicates that you are looking for someone with excellent research and writing skills. My research experience includes . . . and I have had several articles published in the XYZ newsletter."

How much information is too much to include in a cover letter?

Dr. Joan Baum: Don't include more than what is necessary to indicate your willingness and ability to do the job. Do include something about your knowledge of the organization to which you are directing your cover letter and resume, but you need not let everything be known here. A cover letter is an introduction to your resume and both are introductions to get you invited to an interview.

Laura Hill, Managing Director Client Services, Crenshaw Associates, New York, NY: Avoid too many details about why you want to leave (or why you left) your employer.

Liz Ryan: Two paragraphs plus a salutation are the limit. There should be plenty of white space on the page. In the cover letter, you want to show the link between your qualifications and the available job, not repeat everything in your resume.

Karen S. McAndrew: Information that does not add new data or value to your qualifications for the position is probably too much to include in a cover letter. The tone of the letter should demonstrate your enthusiasm for the company and position and can be conveyed with few added words.

Dr. Peter A. Manzi: Anything that takes more than one page is too much! Although some resumes cannot be abridged to be one or even two pages, given a person's long-standing work history, a cover letter should never run longer than a page and, ideally, even less than a full page. It should be a quick summation of what the resume offers. To avoid redundancy, a cover letter need not repeat detailed information found there. A cover letter can use the resume as a reference point for details that highlight a person's achievements. It can also address an issue that may be seen as a barrier, such as, "Please do not let my prior position's salary be a deterrent for consideration."

A cover letter should not contain information about a person's personal or family life, marital status, or other content that an employer cannot legally inquire about in a resume or interview. Cover letters should express why the applicant is interested in the company or organization and convey some current positive knowledge about the company. Company information can be readily obtained from websites and need not be elaborate. Cover letters should always address a specific person and department, and include contact information and any plans to follow up the letter with a call, E-mail, or appearance. Also, a cover letter and resume should always be followed up with a brief printed thank-you letter and a phone or E-mail inquiry about the status of your application.

Evan Burks: Stay away from personal information, and don't reiterate info already on your resume. If you've been referred by someone with a personal connection to the interviewer, this is the time to mention it.

Should I include my E-mail address in my cover letter?

Kathy Woughter: Yes, definitely. It should be part of your heading, just like on your resume.

Evan Burks: Yes, it should be part of your address lines at the top, secondary to your phone number. In the last paragraph, you should also note how the reviewer can reach you.

Bill Coleman, SVP of Compensation, Salary.com, Wellesley, MA: E-mail has become the standard form of communications for many business purposes. Not having an E-mail address can, at best, hinder your chances of getting a reply. Remember, if the hiring person prefers to use E-mail, not having that address available makes it less likely you'll get a response.

However, if you are currently employed, you will probably want to use an E-mail address that does not send messages to your workplace. There are numerous free or inexpensive E-mail services you can use (Hotmail, Yahoo, or most Internet providers). Be cautious in the name you select when registering for an E-mail address that you plan on using for business purposes—keep it professional.

Laura Hill: Yes, your cover letter should have a full header that matches the header on your resume and includes your name, address, phone numbers, and E-mail address.

Tracy Gartmann, Director of the Center for Calling & Career and Director of Placement, Maryville College, Maryville, TN: E-mail has become a very important communication tool for employers and job seekers. Although an employer will most likely use the telephone to initiate contact with you, particularly to schedule your interview, it is common that they may share other information with you over E-mail. Directions to their workplace, a slight change in a meeting place or schedule adjustment—this information is easily communicated via E-mail. In each instance, you need to respond professionally, using your full name, avoiding typographical errors, unnecessary use of exclamation points, and other superfluous punctuation. Your cover letter should have the same style header (which contains your name and contact information) as your resume. This gives your materials a unified and consistent look.

Is a typo on a cover letter a fatal error?

Susan W. Miller: Yes! Proofread your letters carefully for spelling, grammar, and punctuation errors. The letter will be seen as a sample of your writing skills. Also, keep copies of all your correspondence and a record of your follow-up activities.

Is it best to have some letterhead stationery professionally printed for use as cover letters?

Laura Hill: Since many cover letters will be sent via E-mail, stationery is often moot. Send the cover letter as an attachment; use word processing to put your letterhead at the top, matching the heading on your resume. I suggest you buy plain, high-quality paper to print your resume for those occasions when you use traditional mail and for resumes you take with you on interviews.

Evan Burks: No need. You can print it yourself. If you do print a letterhead, don't make the mistake of using unusual type styles, color, or anything that could be deemed less than professional. If you're applying for a "creative" position, a bit more artsy is OK. But that wouldn't be appropriate for a typical business position.

Should I pay a word-processing specialist to type my cover letters?

Karen S. McAndrew: If you have a computer and printer, you can prepare your cover letters without incurring the added expense of paying someone to do it for you. Be sure to use spell check and to have someone whose judgment you value read your cover letter before sending it out.

Evan Burks: Only if you don't have access to word-processing software, Microsoft Word, etc.

Constance Stevens, Career Counselor, Career Paths, Davis, CA: Since you want each resume and cover letter to be focused and tailor made, then I suggest you type your own materials. You would probably be reluctant to edit your cover letter frequently due to the time, bother, and cost of using a specialist. However, if you do not know how to use a computer word processor yet, then a typist may be necessary. However, make sure to make the necessary modifications each time you send out your resume and cover letter. One of the beauties of word processing your own materials is having the ability to customize your approach each time, so you are focused on the reader and that specific position.

An alternative is to have the cover letter originally typed up by a word-processing specialist and then request the file on a floppy disk or as an E-mail attachment. That way, you will have the cover letter already formatted and you can edit it as necessary each time you send it out. Whichever way it gets typed, you need to do a custom job each time.

What is the biggest mistake to avoid in developing my cover letter?

James K. Elkins: As with resumes, the most critical error made in writing cover letters is the failure to mention specific accomplishments. While this will repeat what is on your resume, you should mention only the accomplishments that are recent and relevant to the job for which you are applying. In fact, the cover letter provides you with the opportunity to explain in more detail both the way you solved problems and the benefits resulting.

Martin Jaffe, Manager, InfoPLACE, Cuyahoga County Public Library, Cuyahoga, OH: The key principle in cover letter writing is to focus on the skills and expertise you have and not provide the screener with any information that will be used against you. It is not your burden to give an employer reasons to reject you—your message has to focus on positives rather than screening factors.

For example, here are some of the letters our clients have shown us for critique:

- "My parole officer suggested that employment would be useful to my re-integration to society, and though I spent the last seven years in Folsom prison, I think I could do something useful in your company."

- "During the three years since my layoff as a baker at Tip Top bakery I have often wondered about what it would be like to work as a security officer and I hope you will hire me though I have no experience and never heard of your company I am writing to you."

An effective cover letter tells readers what you have done successfully in the past and what you will do for them in the future: no tales of woe, requests for career counseling, or apologies for lack of education or work history.

Dr. Janet Scarborough, Career Counselor, Bridgeway Career Development, Seattle, WA: Many candidates make the mistake of writing vague generalities that fail to convince the prospective employer that there is a good fit between the job seeker's qualifications and the hiring needs of the organization. From a hiring manager's perspective, employers want to know how adding you to existing staff will make their work lives easier. They are less interested in facts such as your desire to find "challenging work in a dynamic company" because this statement doesn't say anything. Of course you don't want "boring work in a stagnant company!"

Every job seeker should imagine himself or herself as an employer to visualize what the organization needs to be comfortable with a hiring decision. Don't be afraid to let a little personality and creativity show through, but more important, be clear and thorough in demonstrating how your skills and goals are a great match with the requirements of the position being sought.

Evan Burks: Using a "form" letter that does not address the specific situation or sending a letter fraught with errors will typically remove you from any further consideration. If you're trying to sell yourself, yet everything is not perfect, what could the company expect when you're actually performing the job?

How can I make my cover letter as effective as possible?

Dr. Joan Baum: A cover letter should be a complement to the resume. Too often, the cover letter merely repeats in narrative form what is already on the resume. A good principle to keep in mind is that the letters should be fact-filled and indicate what was done. The cover letter should concentrate on filling gaps, providing explanations, emphasizing strong points, addressing interpersonal skills. It should also clearly demonstrate that you have taken the time to find out something about either the company or the field. Clearly, such a cover letter cannot be construed as an all-purpose-to-anyone job request.

Tone is extremely important. Too often, in an effort to sound confident, students sound pompous or simply unreal, as in, "I have excellent communication skills." Much better would be to pat yourself on the back indirectly by putting praise in the form of indirect discourse, for example, "Previous employers have commented on my writing skills, attention to detail, and ability to handle multiple assignments."

Where can I get more information on career planning?

Tracy Gartmann: One of the most helpful tools with regard to career planning and research is the U.S. Department of Labor, Bureau of Labor Statistics *Occupational Outlook Handbook.* Commonly referred to as the "OOH," this resource is online at http://www.bls.gov/oco/home.htm. It lists every job and every industry in the United States, with complete articles about what workers do on the job, working conditions, the training and education needed, earnings, and expected job prospects. It also lists professional organizations associated with particular jobs, which often have websites and electronic employment listings.

Part IV

Cover Letter Examples for Various Positions

The following cover letter examples are separated into groups. The first group contains letters primarily for unskilled and semiskilled positions, for general employment, or for recent college graduates with little or no work experience. Some of these letters are labeled "boilerplate"; you can modify these to suit your needs. The second group contains letters for skilled tradespersons.

The third group contains letters for professional, management, or other upper-level positions. The fourth group contains letters for people in special situations, such as a homemaker, retiree, or veteran returning to the workforce; a Spanish-speaking applicant seeking basic employment; or a former prison inmate. The fifth group contains follow-up letters (very important!) and examples of reference and salary history sheets. And this section ends with additional outstanding cover letters.

ENTRY-LEVEL, SEMISKILLED, OR GENERAL EMPLOYMENT

Use words and phrases from the following examples to write your own, customized cover letter. Remember to research the company whenever possible before calling the hiring authority or writing your letter. When you're prepared to discuss the job opportunity, call the company and try to speak directly to the key decision maker. Tell him or her exactly why you're interested in the firm and, if possible, schedule an interview at that time. If you can't book an interview right away, at least make sure to mention your name clearly to the hiring authority.

Avoid using complex sentences or too many fancy words. Your cover letter will be most effective when you use simple words to communicate important, relevant information. Write at a level your reader can understand and appreciate, and you'll have a much better chance of getting called for an interview.

GENERAL/ENTRY-LEVEL   BOILERPLATE

NANCY J. HARRIS
434 N. Wabash Street
Cleveland, OH 40621
216/555-6845
nharris001@xxx.com

June 3, 20__

Dear Hiring Manager:

I am exploring employment opportunities with your company. Specifically, I am seeking to better utilize my experience and training in [your field of experience/interest].

Throughout my career, I've proven my ability to work effectively with management and staff at all levels of experience. Most important, I can determine and meet the needs of the customer in a professional, yet personalized, manner.

I can provide excellent references upon request and am willing to travel for the right opportunity. Please let me know as soon as possible when we can meet for an interview and discuss mutual interests. I look forward to your response.

Thank you for your time and consideration.

Sincerely,

Nancy J. Harris
enclosure

MIGUEL GARCIA
319 Verde Drive • Denver, CO 30004
303/555-5134 (cell) • mgarcia2@xxx.net

January 21, 20___

Dear Hiring Executive [or Manager]:

I am exploring the possibility of joining your staff and have enclosed my resume for your review. Specifically, I am seeking to better use my talents in [building maintenance, mechanics, professional driving, production operations, etc.].

My background includes training [or experience] in [boiler/HVAC repair; engine rebuilding and tune-ups; on-time deliveries; operation of folders, packers, and cutters; soldering and product assembly; etc.]. I've developed excellent relations with [teachers, managers, co-workers, customers], and I feel that this can be valuable to your firm.

I am available for an interview at your convenience to discuss how my education and experience could benefit your company. Please contact me at the above number or address in order to arrange a meeting. I am looking forward to exploring career opportunities with your company.

Thank you for your time and consideration.

Sincerely,

Miguel Garcia
enclosure

GENERAL/ENTRY-LEVEL BOILERPLATE

LUCY DISH

9876 College Avenue #213
Rockford, IL 60115
815/555-2474 or 555-1540 (cell)
dish22@xxx.com

November 12, 20__

Dear Prospective Employer:

In the interest of exploring employment opportunities with your organization, I have enclosed my resume for your review. Specifically, I am seeking to expand my experience (and training) in [office management, accounting, data processing, etc.].

My strong work ethic and attention to detail would prove extremely valuable to a company that makes customer service its top priority. I am self-motivated and energetic, and communicate well with customers, staff, and management to get the job done.

Please let me know as soon as possible when we can meet to discuss mutual interests. Thank you for your time, and I look forward to your response.

Sincerely,

Lucy Dish
enclosure

GENERAL/ENTRY-LEVEL NEW COLLEGE GRADUATE

CAESAR G. NASH

*21 Wickam Road
Heartland, WI 53029
414/555-5892 (cell)*

May 15, 20___

Dear Hiring Manager:

I am exploring employment opportunities with your company. Specifically, I am seeking to better utilize my ability to train, motivate, and energize both groups and individuals in successful endeavors.

During various volunteer positions in college, I was highly successful in training and coordinating individuals with a wide range of backgrounds. My hands-on work experience includes customer service, sales, and business administration, all with a positive attitude.

I have proven that I can work effectively with management and staff at all levels of experience. Most important, I have demonstrated my ability to determine and meet the needs of the customer in a professional yet personalized manner.

My references are available upon request, and I'm willing to travel for the right opportunity. Please let me know as soon as possible when we can meet for an interview and discuss mutual interests. I look forward to your response.

Thank you for your time and consideration.

Sincerely,

Caesar G. Nash
enclosure

GENERAL/ENTRY-LEVEL NEW COLLEGE GRADUATE

WILLIAM G. STEVENS

21 Nagtown Road • Heartland, WI 53029
414/555-5892 • 414/555-7609 (cell) • wgs23@xxx.net

March 22, 20__

Dear Hiring Manager:

During various volunteer positions in college, I was highly successful in training and coordinating individuals with a wide range of backgrounds. My hands-on work experience includes customer service, sales, and business administration, all with a highly positive attitude.

It was in my Advanced Business class that I first learned of your company, and I would now like to use my ability to train, motivate, and energize groups and individuals in successful endeavors for your company.

Through summer employment, I've proven my ability to work effectively with management and staff at all levels of experience. Most important, I have demonstrated my ability to determine and meet the needs of the customer in a professional, yet personalized, manner.

If required, I can provide excellent references and am willing to travel for the right opportunity. Please let me know as soon as possible when we can meet for an interview and discuss mutual interests. I look forward to your response.

Thank you for your time and consideration.

Sincerely,

William G. Stevens
enclosure

HUNTINGTON CITY-TOWNSHIP
PUBLIC LIBRARY
200 W. Market Street
Huntington, IN 46750

GENERAL/ENTRY-LEVEL   TRUCKING/TRANSPORTATION

ALBERT S. POST
810 Oak Drive #4B
Lisle, IL 60532
708/555-1445 (cell)

August 12, 20__

Dear Hiring Manager:

I am seeking to better utilize my skills in transportation, developed in positions with UPS and Central Transport. As my resume indicates, I have successful experience in many areas of customer service, dock operations, and freight tracking. I'm especially interested in joining a professional, growth-oriented company.

While attending Indiana State University, I was also on the Dean's List, served as assistant coach for the youth hockey team, and was active in the Society for the Advancement of Management. Being involved in these groups helped to round out my education and greatly improved my interpersonal communication skills.

I can provide letters of reference from professors and faculty, and am willing to travel for the right opportunity. Please let me know as soon as possible when we can meet for an interview and discuss mutual interests. I look forward to your response.

Sincerely,

Albert S. Post
enclosure

GENERAL/ENTRY-LEVEL MECHANIC WITH LITTLE TRAINING

GEORGE WEST

1205 Orange Road • Nassau, NY 11736
516/555-0020 (cell) • toolman@xxx.net

September 20, 20__

Dear Hiring Authority:

I am seeking a position as mechanic where I may fully utilize my strong aptitude for working with auto and truck engines, transmissions, and related systems.

My interest in auto mechanics began with intensive training in my high school automotive class, where I learned the basics of repair, troubleshooting, and preventive maintenance.

I've since repaired and completely rebuilt a classic 1973 Chevrolet Camaro, including full teardown and assembly of a 307-cubic-inch small-block engine. I have also worked on a variety of more recent models and am very skilled in all types of general automotive maintenance, including:

• Engine tune-ups, including timing adjustments, belt tightening, spark plug replacement, and replacement of fuel filters and injectors.
• Inspection and filling of all essential fluids, including oil, brake, power steering, and transmission.
• Diagnostic checking and replacement of brake shoes and pads, as well as mufflers, shocks, and struts. This includes some familiarity with advanced computer diagnostics.

In addition to my technical skills, I can bring you a strong work ethic and dependability. I have an excellent record of attendance at my high school. Please feel free to call me with any questions you may have or to arrange a personal interview. I would enjoy meeting with you and your service team.

Thank you for your prompt consideration.

Sincerely,

George West
enclosure

SKILLED TRADESPERSON

With even a small amount of research, you can show the reader why you wish to work for his or her specific company. Remember to address your letter to an individual whenever possible and tell the reader the type of work you're looking for.

In the second paragraph, show points you've learned about the company, its products, facilities, type of operation, etc. Check your resume, job applications, and skill list to emphasize key talents you can bring to the position, especially technical or communication skills sought by the company. Here you can mention such things as proficiency in the use of certain factory equipment or experience at major construction projects.

Finally, request an interview or tell the hiring authority when you'll call, and remember to thank the reader for his or her time and consideration.

SKILLED TRADESPERSON   EQUIPMENT REPAIR

STEVEN FIERO

77 Hill Drive
Bloomingdale, IL 60108
708/555-6370 (cell)

March 11, 20__

Mr. Robert Jones
General Candy Company
5343 Sugar Lane
Sweetbox, IL 60132

Dear Mr. Jones:

I would like to explore employment opportunities with General Candy Company. Specifically, I would like to better utilize my skills in the repair and operation of a wide range of production equipment, developed thus far through my work with American Candy Corporation.

My research has shown that you will soon be expanding your chocolate bar production capacity by nearly 20 percent, and I would like to play a part in your company's success.

As you will see by my resume, my background includes full responsibility for equipment teardown and troubleshooting. I've proven my ability to work closely with staff and management in plant safety and production streamlining, while keeping an eye on overhead. I have an excellent record of attendance and efficiency, and can provide you with references upon request.

Please let me know as soon as possible when we can meet for an interview. I look forward to your response.

Thank you for your time and consideration.

Sincerely,

Steven Fiero
enclosure

SKILLED TRADESPERSON PHOTOCOPIER REPAIR

KATIE MELENDEZ
P.O. Box 2334
Orlando, FL 32802
(407) 555-2994 (day)
(407) 555-3077 (evening)

April 8, 20__

Dear Personnel Representative:

Given the excellent reputation of Savin Corporation, I have enclosed my resume for your review.

My background includes full responsibility for the teardown, repair, and troubleshooting of virtually all brands of photocopiers to component level. In addition, I have:

◆ Recently completed training in digital copier technology.
◆ Successfully trained several employees in direct customer service, system repair, and documentation.
◆ Earned numerous commendations from customers and supervisors for prompt, effective repairs and reduced service calls.

Throughout my career, I've proven my ability to quickly learn new photocopier systems and to always stay abreast of the latest technologies. I believe this is essential for keeping positive relations with all customers, while reducing both downtime and overhead costs.

I would welcome the chance to meet with you or your technical staff to discuss career opportunities. Please let me know as soon as possible when I could come to your office for an interview.

Sincerely,

Katie Melendez
enclosure

SKILLED TRADESPERSON MACHINIST/SHOP WORKER

DOYLE LYONS

228 Magnolia Avenue, Apartment 18   (909) 425-6769 (cell)
Riverside, CA 92506   dlyons@xxx.com

October 25, 20__

Dear Hiring Manager:

With extensive training in shop operations and more than two years of experience as a machinist, I am certain I can bring your company the skills and devotion to quality required for success.

I have successful experience in lathe, mill, and grinding work for jigs, fixtures, prototypes, and one-of-a-kind products. This includes both traditional and computer-controlled systems.

My background includes full responsibility for job scheduling and supervision, from blueprint reading to finished product quality and customer satisfaction. I can handle a wide range of production duties while reducing waste and overhead costs.

I would welcome the opportunity to meet with you personally regarding your specific shop needs. I can provide references upon request and look forward to hearing from you soon.

Sincerely,

Doyle Lyons

enclosure

SKILLED TRADESPERSON WELDER

Tim Caine

56 Carson Street
Murphy, NC 28906
(828) 555-8865
(828) 320-0205 (mobile)
cainefamily@xxx.net

July 1, 20__

Dear Hiring Manager:

Given the solid reputation of your company, I am exploring opportunities as a maintenance welder. As a reliable member of your production team, I can offer your company proficiency in:

— ARC, MIG, TIG, Flux-core, and gas welding for a wide range of products and maintenance welding applications.
— Full project supervision, including welding, assembly, and quality control.
— A strong aptitude for learning how to operate new equipment, while keeping a sharp eye on the quality of the finished product.

Because the enclosed resume is only a brief outline of my skills and abilities, I would welcome the chance to meet with you personally and to discuss the needs of your particular operation and tell you all that I have to offer.

I can provide excellent references upon request and am willing to travel for the right opportunity. Please let me know as soon as possible when we can meet for an interview. I look forward to your response.

Thank you for your time and consideration.

Sincerely,

Tim Caine
enclosure

SKILLED TRADESPERSON CASINO WORKER

ALEX GUTIERREZ

344 NORTH ROCKWELL CANYON • VALENCIA, CA 91355
(661) 459-8936 (CELL) • ALEX23@XXX.COM

February 11, 20__

Mr. Ralph Albertson
Hollywood Casinos
49 West Galena Blvd.
Aurora, CA 43211

Dear Mr. Albertson:

According to a recent article in the *San Francisco Chronicle*, your casino will soon be expanding its operations. I would like to meet with you or your staff to discuss career opportunities with your successful organization.

My background includes experience as crewman with Fleetwide Marine Corporation. With my knowledge of food and beverage service and management, along with my crewman's experience and Sanitation Certification, I would be a versatile professional aboard your vessel.

As my resume indicates, I have extensive experience in business administration, including staff training, supervision, and the coordination of daily operations. In addition, I am qualified in job scheduling, as well as material and supply purchasing.

I can provide excellent references for your review. I am willing to travel or relocate for the right opportunity. Please let me know as soon as possible when we can meet to discuss any crewman or service position available. I look forward to your response.

Thank you for your time and consideration.

Sincerely,

Alex Gutierrez
enclosure

SKILLED TRADESPERSON TRAVEL AGENT

Lisa Marie Hardy
139 Washington Road
Westminster, MD 21157
(410) 366-7212

September 13, 20__

Dear Hiring Manager:

I can bring your travel agency the strict attention to detail and solid communication skills that are essential to success. My background includes hands-on training and experience in direct customer service, reservations, itinerary planning, and problem solving. Most important, I can provide:

• Successful experience in customer service, CRT work, and telephone communications.
• An excellent knowledge of airline rates, routes, and ground services.
• The ability to solve customer problems in a prompt, personalized manner.

I am willing to travel or relocate for the right opportunity and could meet to discuss mutual interests.

Thank you for your time and consideration.

Sincerely,

Lisa Marie Hardy
enclosure

SKILLED TRADESPERSON DRAFTING/DESIGN

Barry Hamdi

3402 Congress Avenue, MS #127 • Lake Worth, FL 33461
(561) 439-7033 • (561) 439-1640 (cell) • barryhamdi@xxx.com

June 29, 20__

Dear Hiring Manager:

My strong attention to detail and aptitude for learning have been the keys to my success at Lakeworth Community College, where I recently completed my Associate's Degree in Architectural Drafting and Design. I now would like to utilize my training and skills in either a full-time or apprentice position with your excellent company.

I have consistently demonstrated my ability to learn the latest in computer software while fine-tuning my communication/research skills. Because my resume is only a summary of my background, I would welcome the opportunity to meet with you personally to discuss your specific business operation. I can provide excellent references upon request and look forward to a personal interview at your convenience.

Thank you for your time and consideration.

Sincerely yours,

Barry Hamdi

encl.

SKILLED TRADESPERSON LEAD COOK/CHEF

CHARLES GROVES

508 East Huron Drive   Ann Arbor, MI 48103
(313) 720-4388 (cell)   grovesfamily@xxx.net.

December 3, 20__

Dear Hiring Manager:

Having held positions as kitchen manager and sous-chef with restaurants such as Chez Paul, I am certain I can be an asset to your operation. Specifically, I am seeking to better utilize my skills in staff motivation and supervision in a high-quality restaurant, where service and professionalism are the keys to success.

My background includes full responsibility for kitchen operations and sanitation. During my position with Chez Paul, I developed a strong repeat business through strict attention to detail and quality. This resulted in highly favorable reviews in such publications as *The Michelin Guide* and the *Chicago Tribune*.

Prior to Chez Paul, as my resume indicates, I was sous-chef at Prairie Restaurant, which specialized in American and French cuisine. It was here that I fine-tuned my skills in creative presentations and hearty entrees.

Please let me know as soon as possible when we can discuss how my skills can help enhance your reputation.

Thank you for your time and consideration.

Sincerely,

Charles Groves
enclosure

SKILLED TRADESPERSON AUTOMOBILE SALES

Tavonya Adams

P.O. Box 1332

Knoxville, TN 37933-1332

(865) 539-4867 (day)

(865) 668-3718 (evening)

tavonya@xxx.net

August 11, 20__

Dear Hiring Manager:

With more than seven years in automobile sales, I am seeking to better utilize my experience in automotive sales management, developed in various positions with such dealerships as Knoxville Motors and Rocky Top Ford.

- My background includes full responsibility for department setup and management, as well as effective closed-door sales. I'm a strong believer in supervision by example, and have proven my ability to motivate workers and increase sales of new and used automobiles, warranties, and after-market products.
- I was directly responsible for over $1.6 million in gross sales for 2002.
- Throughout my career, I have proven my ability to expand dealership sales through positive, personalized service to a wide range of clientele.

Please let me know as soon as possible when we can meet for an interview and discuss opportunities for increased profitability at your dealership. I look forward to your response.

Thank you for your time and consideration.

Sincerely,

Tavonya Adams
encl.

SKILLED TRADESPERSON   HVAC SERVICE/INSTALLER

John V. Landisberg
P.O. Box 122 • Twin Falls, ID 83303
(208) 555-4338 • (208) 555-3477 (fax) • johnnyl@xxx.com

January 28, 20__

Dear Hiring Manager:

Given the expanding housing market in our portion of the state, the demand for quality HVAC installations and repair has never been greater. I recently received certification in HVAC systems and am certain my education in state-of-the-art equipment can benefit your customers and your company.

My training from Triton College, where I attended until recently relocating in Twin Falls, has given me expertise in:

- Assessment of heating and cooling needs for residential and commercial structures of up to 100,000 cubic feet.
- The teardown and troubleshooting of air conditioners, gas and electric furnaces, and a wide range of other equipment, including humidifiers.
- Dealing with vendors and parts suppliers to tackle custom work with speed and consistently high quality, at the lowest possible cost.

Throughout my employment as a handyman at a small apartment complex, I've proven my ability to work well with customers and provide quick, professional service. I am very self-motivated, with an excellent record of attendance and customer satisfaction.

Please let me know as soon as possible when we can meet for an interview and discuss in detail how my skills can benefit you. I look forward to your response. Thank you for your time and consideration.

Sincerely,

John V. Landisberg
enclosure

SKILLED TRADESPERSON   GENERAL OFFICE/ADMINISTRATION

Michelle Peterson
600 Dufferin Street
King City, ONT L7B B3
(416) 377-6077 (day)
(416) 552-3884 (evening)

May 22, 20__

Elm Street Doctors Complex
14 Bobbit Avenue
King City, ONT L7B 1B4

Dear Hiring Physician:

Today's office environment requires speed, accuracy, and strict attention to detail. These are among the many qualifications I can bring to your practice. Specifically, I would like to better utilize my experience in direct patient relations and office administration.

As my resume indicates, I have extensive experience in patient scheduling, billing, and general bookkeeping. Throughout my employment and education, I've developed a strong background in medical/dental terminology and clinical procedures, essential elements in effective patient care.

Most important, I have proven my ability to determine and meet the needs of the patient in a professional yet personalized manner.

I would like to meet for an interview to discuss mutual interests and can be reached after 6 P.M. on weekdays at the above phone number. I look forward to your response.

Thank you for your time and consideration.

Sincerely,

Michelle Peterson
encl.

SKILLED TRADESPERSON OFFICE/SALES ADMINISTRATION

Amber Keese

788 Richards Avenue, Apartment B
Norwalk, CT 06854
(203) 555-6820
amberk@xxx.com

May 3, 20__

Dear Hiring Manager:

My profit-building skills in sales administration, market expansion, and product development could prove highly valuable to a growing, innovative company such as yours.

My background includes the establishment of highly profitable territories, as well as all aspects of product configuration and account management for the sale of household goods. I believe I can improve your company's profitability through market penetration, sales staff training, and/or overall sales management. During my most recent position, I:

- Achieved a 15 percent growth in sales among soft product lines.
- Developed a strong referral business through personalized service, quick troubleshooting, and excellent product knowledge.

Because my resume is necessarily brief, I would welcome the chance to meet with you personally regarding your specific operation and discuss how my skills can expand your market share. I am willing to travel for the right opportunity and can provide excellent client references at your request.

Thank you for your time and consideration. I look forward to meeting with you soon.

Sincerely,

Amber Keese
enclosure

SKILLED TRADESPERSON   CLERK/OFFICE ASSISTANT

Mark L. Hall

230B Claremont Drive • Batavia, OH 45103
(513) 555-7802 (day) • (513) 555-4495 (evening)
mlh22@xxx.com

July 28, 20__

Mr. John Richards
Richards & Associates
390 E. Jackson Road
Batavia, OH 45103

Dear Mr. Richards:

I am exploring opportunities as an office assistant, and your advertisement in the *Batavia News* seems perfectly matched to my qualifications. I can bring your company comprehensive analytical and communication skills, as well as a background in data entry and retrieval.

As my resume indicates, I have direct experience in cash applications and account reconciliation, as well as a solid background in customer communications and problem solving. I've proven my ability to quickly learn new procedures, while streamlining operations for prompt, accurate customer response.

I can provide excellent references on request and am willing to travel for the right opportunity. Please let me know as soon as possible when we can meet for an interview and discuss mutual interests. I look forward to your response.

Thank you for your time and consideration.

Sincerely,

Mark L. Hall
encl.

Brenda Givens

744 Newmark Road
Coos Bay, OR 97420
(541) 555-2998
(541) 555-1202 (cell)
bgivens@xxx.net

October 6, 20__

Dear Hiring Manager:

Effective customer service is essential to the success of any organization, and I am exploring new opportunities to utilize my experience to benefit your company.

My background includes responsibility for the training and supervision of customer service staff at Northwest Lakes Resort. It was here that I fine-tuned my skills in data entry, sales support, and a wide range of office functions. I now seek to better utilize my talents in a challenging environment offering professional growth and stability.

I've proven my ability to use tact and professionalism in working with staff and management and, most important, with virtually all types of customers.

Please let me know as soon as possible when we can meet to discuss mutual interests or if you require any further information on my background. I look forward to hearing from you soon.

Sincerely,

Brenda Givens
enclosure

SKILLED TRADESPERSON ADMINISTRATIVE ASSISTANT

Sally Haga
788 DeKalb Pike
Blue Bell, PA 19422
(215) 641-6559 (cell)
sally32@xxx.net

February 19, 20__

Edwin Albertson
Vice President
Tri-Cities Electrical Corporation
P.O. Box 233
Blue Bell, PA 19422

Dear Mr. Albertson:

    I am exploring opportunities as administrative assistant and heard about your company through Roger Leech, who suggested I send you my resume.

    I am a skilled typist, proficient in both Word and WordPerfect. As my resume indicates, I have highly successful experience in the medical field and with Sears Roebuck. Throughout my career, I've proven my ability to work effectively with management and staff at all levels of experience. Most important, I can ensure high customer satisfaction through personalized yet effective communications.

    I am eager to join your successful team of professionals. Please let me know as soon as possible when we may meet for an interview and discuss mutual interests. I look forward to your response.

    Thank you for your time and consideration.

Sincerely,

Sally Haga

enclosure

SKILLED TRADESPERSON   AIRCRAFT TECHNICIAN/MECHANIC

GLENN PROVENZANO
1320 Washington Avenue • Tucker, GA 30085
770/555-7032 • 770/555-4533 (cell)

April 17, 20__

Mr. Ted B. Sample
President
XYZ Corporation
800 Enterprise Drive, Suite 209
Atlanta, GA 30328

Dear Mr. Sample:

During my military tenure, I saved the Air Force a $1,000 overhaul cost per brake assembly and improved the repair capability at the various shops to which I was assigned. In addition, I developed and successfully administered a nondestructive inspection program. I thrive on the challenge of improving both productivity and systems. I am goal-oriented and professional, and I would like to put my experience to work for you.

If it is required, please forward an employment application in the enclosed self-addressed, stamped envelope. My credentials include:

• Airframe Mechanic License.

• More than seven years of military aviation experience, including positions as crew chief and aircraft hydraulic technician/mechanic.

• Completion of the Aviation Maintenance Technology program through Embryo-Riddle Aeronautical University.

• For Outstanding Service and Excellent Performance, I received two Air Force Achievement Medals and one Air Force Commendation Medal.

I'm confident that with my mechanical and technical skills, I would be a valuable asset and could offer many years of quality service. I appreciate your time and look forward to discussing my qualifications in a personal interview.

Sincerely,

Glenn Provenzano
enclosure

SKILLED TRADESPERSON—SHIPPING/RECEIVING

Jennifer Pope
305 Hunter Boulevard
Regina, Saskatchewan S4P 3E1
(306) 588-3448
jhpope@xxx.net

March 23, 20__

Mr. Robert Smith
Smith and Hebert, Inc.
100 E. Smith St.
Regina, Saskatchewan S4P 3E1

Dear Mr. Smith:

I am exploring new opportunities in distribution and/or shipping operations with your company. Specifically, I would like to utilize my experience with EBM in a challenging new position.

My employment with EBM has greatly expanded my skills in routing, trafficking, and distribution, and I've gained an excellent knowledge of freight carriers, rates, and delivery schedules. Throughout my career, I've proven my ability to work effectively with management and staff at all levels of experience. Most important, I have demonstrated my ability to determine and meet the needs of the customer in fast-paced business environments.

I will be calling you early next week to arrange an interview. Please let me know if there's any further information you require regarding my skills and how they can be tailored to meet your specific needs. I look forward to meeting you soon.

Thank you for your time and consideration.

Sincerely,

Jennifer Pope
enclosure

SKILLED TRADESPERSON SECURITY GUARD

WILLIAM E. WINKLER
432 E. Amelia • Denver, CO 80202
303/555-0170 (day) • 303/555-7622 (evening) • wwinkler@xxx.net

July 31, 20__

Dear Hiring Manager:

A consistent rise in theft at retail operations nationwide prompts me to enclose my resume for your review. I am exploring opportunities in retail security, and would like to better utilize my experience in safety, shortage, and security operations, developed with Venture Stores, Inc.

My background includes full responsibility for suspect surveillance and apprehension, and I have proven my ability to work effectively with staff and management at all levels of experience. Most important, I have demonstrated my ability to reduce lost revenues from theft or shrinkage, while maintaining a safe environment for all employees and customers.

I can provide letters of recommendation from managers. Please let me know as soon as possible when we can meet for an interview to discuss how my skills can help your company lower its losses. I look forward to your response.

Thank you for your time and consideration.

Sincerely,

William E. Winkler
encl.

PROFESSIONAL/MANAGEMENT

The following examples are for professional and/or management positions requiring special skills, training, or a college degree. You should write your letter at a level appropriate for the employer or position. In other words, don't be afraid to use industry-specific terminology that demonstrates how well you understand the position you're seeking. Employers at this level need to see that you have a good command of the language and that you can write with precision and impact. This is especially true if the job itself will require writing reports, memos, or information related to customers or products.

While writing your cover letter, always think about how relevant your material is to the position you are seeking. What are the most important aspects of your background that will pry open the door to an interview and get you noticed for a specific job? This is the kind of information employers want to see in the first one or two paragraphs of your cover letter.

PROFESSIONAL/MANAGEMENT MANUFACTURING/DESIGN ENGINEERING

Donald A. Crane

55 Justin Court   Vienna, VA 22182
703/555-7215   703/555-6632 (cell)
doncrane@xxx.com

October 21, 20__

Ms. Naomi Justin
PBT Enterprises
1501 Duke Street
Alexandria, VT 22314

Dear Ms. Justin,

With more than twelve years in manufacturing and design engineering,
I would like to discuss how my experience can benefit your company.
I most recently read about your company's acquisition of Atalan, Inc.,
a former client of my employer, GS Gibson.

I currently manage a design and manufacturing engineering team in
state-of-the-art product and process development for a wide range of
applications. I would be most valuable to you in a position requiring
greater innovation and creativity, and that offers the potential for career
advancement.

My efforts have resulted in major cost reductions and quality improve-
ments for key customers, as well as for in-house operations. I can now
assist your technical staff in virtually all stages of process
and product development.

I can provide much more information, including a portfolio of photo-
graphs of my most important work. To that end, I look forward to hearing
from you soon.

Sincerely,

Donald A. Crane
enclosure

PROFESSIONAL/MANAGEMENT **BUSINESS ADMINISTRATION**

MARK J. DAVIDSON
774 Smithfield Drive
Cleveland, OH 44130
440/555-9783
440/555-6558 (cell)

August 12, 20__

Mr. Richard Carter
American Charter Co.
650 E. Broad St.
Cleveland, OH 44132

Dear Mr. Carter

With more than six years of success in business administration and operations, I feel certain I can increase your company's profitability.

My background includes full responsibility for cost-effective purchasing, vendor relations, and inventory control on state-of-the-art computer systems. I'm also skilled in general accounting, bookkeeping, and payroll operations. If necessary, I can train and motivate a team of workers in a professional manner.

Because this letter and resume give only an outline of my background, I welcome the chance to meet with you personally to discuss your particular business needs. To that end, I will be contacting you soon to arrange an interview.

Thank you for your time and consideration.

Sincerely,

Mark J. Davidson

encl.

PROFESSIONAL/MANAGEMENT PROJECT MANAGER

JOHN MIDDLETON

810 East Palm Drive ◆ Rockford, IL 61107
815/555-1804 ◆ 815/555-2337 (cell) ◆ johnmiddle@xxx.com

November 21, 20__

Mr. Jim Richardson
JWP Kenyon Electric Company
P.O. Box 1772
Rockford, IL 61106

Dear Mr. Richardson:

I would like to meet with you to discuss opportunities as project manager. As you will see on review of the enclosed resume, I have both field and office experience on a wide variety of projects, including crew supervision at the Smith-Case Building at 400 East Main Street.

My background includes assisting in full job estimating and project management, and I would like to further my formal education in these subjects. The foremen and journeymen I've worked with will tell you that I'm very self-motivated, ambitious, and quick to learn new procedures.

Because my resume is only a summary of my background, I would welcome the opportunity to meet with you personally to discuss mutual interests. Thanks for your consideration, and I look forward to hearing from you soon.

Sincerely,

John Middleton
enclosure

PROFESSIONAL/MANAGEMENT CONSTRUCTION MANAGER

ROBERT L. AUGUSTA
806 Fisher Lane • Clark, NJ 07066
908/555-0627 (day) • 908/555-7855 (evening)
r_augusta@xxx.com

April 24, 20__

Dear Hiring Manager:

I am currently employed by a major, nationwide remodeling company. This company was recently voted Re-modeler of the Year for the entire country by a very respected industry publication. I held the position of installation manager in the New Jersey branch and have contributed in making possible this honor.

My background includes responsibility for up to 25 projects simultaneously, using knowledge and experience gained in my company's 44 years in the business. I now seek to further my career with a company that can provide even greater responsibility and growth potential. In turn, I can offer my new employer the dedication, enthusiasm, and commitment required in such a position.

I am an extremely independent worker who is at his best under pressure. I am very well liked by my fellow workers, subcontractors, and suppliers. I like to think that I am personally responsible for helping create a very high-energy, positive work environment. This positive atmosphere creates a very productive and, in turn, profitable business. I love to deal with people and take pride in accomplishing big projects and solving problems. I feel great when I can save my employer money and am always looking to take on more, learn more, and be more valuable to my company.

I would appreciate a personal interview with your firm. Given the chance for an interview, I will be glad to explain more fully the ways I could be an extremely valuable asset to your organization.

I look forward to hearing from you.

Sincerely,

Robert L. Augusta
encl.

CASEY M. JONES
61 Ramsgate Circle North
Burlington, Ontario L7N 3H8
905/555-4484 (cell)

March 9, 20__

Dear Hiring Manager:

In this uncertain economy, even in the best-managed companies, there is a growing consensus that experienced manufacturing talent will prove key to profitable operations throughout the coming decade.

Through 20 years of proven success, I've demonstrated a consistent ability to contribute to profitability in all areas of production, process engineering, and leadership.

By way of example, as plant manager for a specialty metal products company, I've been instrumental in managing growth from $18 million to more than $40 million in a relatively short period of time. However, for reasons that I would be glad to share privately, I am looking to explore some new challenges.

Because I feel that your situation is one where my experience would fit nicely, I decided to forward my resume. If in reviewing it, you feel it merits at least an exploratory discussion, I would like to arrange a visit at your convenience.

My thanks in advance for your consideration. I look forward to your response.

Sincerely,

Casey M. Jones
enclosure

PROFESSIONAL/MANAGEMENT STAFF REGISTERED NURSE

SAMUEL LYONS
6484 West Mason Street
San Francisco, CA 94103
(415) 555-3792 (day)
(415) 555-4424 (evening)
samlyons@xxx.net

June 20, 20__

Ms. Nellie DeVille
Supervisor of Nursing
Citizens Hospital
P.O. Box 2150
Denver, CO 80202

Dear Ms. DeVille:

I am seeking to relocate to Colorado and fully utilize my experience as staff RN. I have already applied for my Colorado nursing license and am available immediately to discuss career opportunities with you.

My background includes experience in cardiac monitoring and med-surg tele units, where I developed my skills in triage, phlebotomy, and overall patient care. I am very self-motivated and am interested in pursuing graduate studies in nursing during night courses (unless you have night shifts available).

Throughout my career, I've proven my ability to work effectively with physicians and staff at all levels of experience. Most important, I have demonstrated my ability to promptly meet patient needs with a highly professional yet personalized approach.

I can provide excellent references upon request. Please let me know as soon as possible when we can meet for an interview and discuss mutual interests. I look forward to your response.

Thank you for your time and consideration.

Sincerely,

Samuel Lyons
enclosure

PROFESSIONAL/MANAGEMENT SALES/MARKETING

YVONNE BACKARA

3350 Newcastle Drive   Seattle, WA 98119
Office: 206/555-6090   Residence: 206/555-8195
Cell: 206/555-2422

March 1, 20__

Sales Manager
Widget-Makers, Inc.
50 Safeway Drive
Seattle, WA 98118

Dear Sales Manager:

Having reviewed your most recent quarterly report, I am sending my resume and would like to explore opportunities in sales and marketing with your excellent company. Your 20 percent sales growth in 2002–2003 tells me that your product and client services are filling a strong need, a need I can help meet while expanding your profits and market share.

My background includes full responsibility for sales presentations and marketing program development. In my most recent position with Xerox, I have:

➤ Personally acquired over 43 new accounts, three of which are Fortune 500 firms.
➤ Earned three Golden Arch awards for exceeding sales goals by over 15 percent for three months in 2002.
➤ Trained and supervised 12 new sales representatives, two of whom earned Golden Arch awards.

Please let me know as soon as possible when we may meet to discuss how my self-motivation and high-energy sales techniques can help improve your company's bottom line. I look forward to your response.

Thank you for your time and consideration.

Sincerely,

Yvonne Backara
enclosure

PROFESSIONAL/MANAGEMENT SALES OR MARKETING MANAGEMENT

DONALD E. TILAN
434 Hillcrest Drive
Jacksonville, FL 32207
904/555-3544 (cell)
tilandon@xxx.com

February 16, 20__

Sales Manager
Fieldcrest Products
12761 Enterprise Dr.
Fort Myers, FL 33908

Dear Sales Manager:

I am exploring opportunities in sales or marketing management with
your company. Specifically, I am seeking to better utilize my profit-
building experience, which includes:

• The highly profitable acquisition and management of major national
  accounts, including WalMart, Home Depot, and KMart.
• Sales staff hiring, training, and supervision; dealer network establishment; and full P&L responsibility for product development, introduction, and marketing.
• Cost reduction, budgeting, forecasting, materials control, purchasing,
  and complete business startup and management.

Because the enclosed resume is necessarily a summary statement,
I would welcome the opportunity to meet with you personally to discuss
how my qualifications may be tailored to meet your specific needs.

Please let me know as soon as possible when we can meet. I look forward to your response.

Sincerely,

Donald E. Tilan
enclosure

PROFESSIONAL/MANAGEMENT FIELD SALES/SERVICE REP

KELLY JONES
263 Newport Drive • Atlanta, GA 30309
404/555-1704 • 404/555-4322 (cell)

June 24, 20__

Nancy Andrews
M&M Mars, Inc.
520 N. Michigan #810, Dept. PC
Atlanta, GA 30312

Dear Ms. Andrews:

I am exploring opportunities as a sales representative with M&M Mars. My present territory includes the Far West Suburbs, and the position you have advertised seems perfect for me. Specifically, I would like to better utilize my self-motivation and profit-building skills.

As a buyer with Jewel Discount Grocery, I worked directly with M&M Mars to coordinate seasonal and holiday promotions, and thus I'm very familiar with your product line. My experience includes major account development, and I've proven my ability to develop strong working relationships with major retailers, including Cub Foods and Wallace Drug. Previous employers have said that I'm reliable, dependable, and efficient, and I believe my track record of success bears out this belief.

Because my resume is necessarily a summary statement, I would welcome the opportunity to meet with you personally to discuss your particular business needs. To that end, I look forward to hearing from you soon.

Thank you for your time and consideration.

Sincerely,

Kelly Jones
enclosure

PROFESSIONAL/MANAGEMENT PUBLIC RELATIONS/COMMUNICATIONS

PAULA CLINE
136 Techway Drive ❖ Chicago, IL 60611
312/555-9449 (day) ❖ 312/555-6833 (evening) ❖ pcline@xxx.net

May 12, 20__

Manager
Public Relations Dept.
McQuirty & Co.
Evansville, IN 47715

Dear Hiring Manager:

As Director of the Alliance Against Intoxicated Motorists (AAIM), I've developed excellent relationships with key decision makers at major businesses, as well as in local and state government. These individuals have included leaders ranging from the Illinois Secretary of State to the DuPage County State's Attorney. This networking was achieved through extensive negotiations to pass new legislation, modify existing laws, or expand public awareness on important safety issues.

Given the obvious success of your firm, I would now like to apply my experience as an active member of your team. I am seeking a position where I may fully utilize my expertise in government relations, public affairs, and/or communications.

Throughout my career, I've proven my ability to generate publicity and handle scores of interviews with print and electronic media. I have researched and written persuasive articles for local and national publications, while testifying before committees and managing a wide range of PR functions for AAIM.

I am willing to travel for the right opportunity and will be calling you soon to arrange a personal interview. Meanwhile, please let me know if there is any further information you require.

Thank you for your time and consideration.

Yours truly,

Paula Cline
enclosure

PROFESSIONAL/MANAGEMENT   INTERNAL PROMOTION OPPORTUNITY

ROBERTA B. KENT
808 Camden Avenue
Carson City, NV 89701
775/555-7564
775/555-0860 (cell)
robkent@xxx.net

October 30, 20__

Dr. Werner Frederick
Postalia, GmbH
Emmentaler Strasse 132
3000 Berlin 51
FEDERAL REPUBLIC OF GERMANY

Dear Dr. Frederick:

Enclosed is my resume outlining my experience and responsibilities with our company. My career with Postalia has been very rewarding, and I now seek greater responsibilities in divisional management.

My position as National Dealer Manager requires an extensive knowledge of our dealer network. I've utilized this expertise to develop a strong camaraderie among our sales representatives, dealers, and customers alike. Through personal rapport building, communications, and motivation, my sales teams have proven to be among the best in the company.

With a strong sense of the internal and external needs of Postalia, I am confident that my talents will be an excellent resource in the years ahead. I would therefore appreciate a meeting at your convenience to discuss mutual interests.

Thank you for your time and consideration, Dr. Frederick, and I look forward to speaking with you at your earliest convenience.

Sincerely,

Roberta B. Kent
encl.

PROFESSIONAL/MANAGEMENT   INSURANCE

EDNA PEARSON

923 Aurora Avenue
Phoenix, AZ 85009-9987
(480) 555-8823
(480) 555-3323 (cell)
epearson2@xxx.com

January 15, 20___

Dear Hiring Manager:

My career as agency manager with AllState Insurance has provided excellent experience in operations management, sales development, and staff supervision. I'm now seeking to increase the profitability of your company.

Throughout my career, I have demonstrated my skills in staff training, motivation, and team building. With AllState Insurance, this has resulted in greatly expanded market share and sales volume. I achieved this by keeping a constant, sharp eye on customer service, follow-up, and the three most important areas of business success: persistence, productivity, and profitability.

I am willing to travel or relocate for the right opportunity and can provide excellent references at your request. Please let me know as soon as possible when we can meet to discuss mutual interests. I look forward to hearing from you soon.

Sincerely,

Edna Pearson

enclosure

PROFESSIONAL/MANAGEMENT ACCOUNTING/FINANCE

ALBERT T. LEKEN
24 Homewood Drive
Vail, CO 81658
970/555-5636
970/555-8355 (cell)

November 11, 20__

Ms. Donna Pearson
Vice President, Finance
Helmand & Pratt
Aspen, CO 81611

Dear Ms. Pearson,

I am exploring opportunities in accounting or finance with your company. Specifically, I would like to utilize my leadership skills in a challenging position that offers the potential for advancement.

My background includes full responsibility for audits and status reporting. In my current position, I've proven my ability to cut costs by 20 percent, while working with staff from all departments in a strong team atmosphere. I am certain I can help improve your accounting functions while increasing your company's bottom-line profitability.

I would welcome the chance to meet you personally and discuss the needs of your business. I can provide excellent references upon request. I look forward to speaking with you soon.

Thank you for your time and consideration.

Yours truly,

Albert T. Leken
encl.

PROFESSIONAL/MANAGEMENT CAD/CAM DRAFTING AND DESIGN

FARIDA C. PATEL
18 Westing Apartments, #9 • Trenton, NJ 08625
609/555-7431 • 609/555-5534 (cell)

November 17, 20__

Ms. Susan Folke
Architect Design Services
200 W. 25th St.
New York, NY 10017

Dear Ms. Folke,

A recent article in *Industry Week* magazine outlines your company's state-of-the-art approach to the design of customized parts for the automotive industry. Yours is the type of company I would like to be associated with. I can bring a creative, self-motivated attitude to your design team, as well as:

- Education and experience in AUTOCAD and Microstation/Intergraph systems.
- Skills in producing prompt, accurate computer conversions of manually drafted blueprints and schematics.
- A strong track record of reliability and success at my most recent position, as well as the ability to interface with staff, managers, and end-users at all levels.

I have proven my ability to work with engineers, technical staff, and managers at virtually all levels of experience. Perhaps most important, I have fine-tuned my ability to learn new systems and procedures quickly and accurately, while keeping a sharp eye on customer satisfaction and quality.

Please let me know as soon as possible when we can meet for an interview and discuss mutual interests. I look forward to your response.

Thank you for your time and consideration.

Sincerely,

Farida C. Patel
encl.

PROFESSIONAL/MANAGEMENT LAW ENFORCEMENT

JANE FATICA
820 Wesley Drive
Pierre, SD 57501
605/555-6803 (day)
605/555-4432 (evening)
faticaj@xxx.net

February 8, 20__

Mayor John Custis
City of Santa Monica
Santa Monica, CA 90403

Dear Mayor Custis:

I am exploring opportunities as police chief with your department. Specifically, I am seeking to utilize my extensive background in law enforcement development with the Pierre Police Department.

In addition to more than 10 years of on-the-job experience, I can offer extensive training and certificates and commendations for professional service. Throughout my career, I have proven my ability to work with fellow officers and the community to investigate and solve a wide range of crimes. Most important, I have fine-tuned my communication skills with the public to help gain its essential support for law enforcement.

Complete documentation of my training, commendations, and service will be provided at your request. Please let me know as soon as possible when we can meet for an interview and discuss the needs of your department.

Thank you for your time and consideration.

Sincerely,

Jane Fatica
enclosure

PROFESSIONAL/MANAGEMENT EDUCATION/TEACHING

SAMUEL E. BURCH

P.O. Box 2234
Helena, MT 59604

406/555-8649
406/555-6654 (cell)

October 25, 20__

Dr. Kenneth Markus
Asst. Superintendent for Administrative Services
Helena School District
466 Newbury Drive
Helena, MT 59604

Dear Dr. Markus,

Thank you for the opportunity to be a substitute teacher in your excellent school district. I am eager to continue my teaching endeavors at Hoover High School as a full-time teacher in the Social Science Department.

Throughout my education and numerous teaching experiences, I have proven my strong, natural skills as a teacher of history on the secondary level. My American history student teaching experience at South Helena High School, under the supervision of Steven Hester, further confirms my effectiveness in determining and meeting student needs. In addition, I can communicate with parents regarding the special needs of their children and how to meet those needs.

My qualifications are presented in more detail on the enclosed resume, and your human services office has my completed job application on file. I can provide excellent references and credentials upon request.

Please contact me as soon as possible to discuss when we can meet for an interview. I look forward to your response.

Thank you for your time and consideration.

Yours truly,

Samuel E. Burch
encl.

PROFESSIONAL/MANAGEMENT OCCUPATIONAL SAFETY

CHARLES WILSON
518 Darst Street
Dublin, VA 24084
(540) 555-1859
Cell: (540) 555-2330
E-mail: cjwilson@xxx.com

May 27, 20__

Jane F. Anderson, Director of Human Resources
Tri-City Manufacturing
P.O. Box 227
Atlanta, GA 30339

Dear Ms. Anderson:

Please accept the enclosed resume in application for the position of Director of Plant Safety as advertised on your company's website.

I think you will find that my extensive background in occupational safety meets or exceeds the qualifications for this position. While serving as assistant safety director for a large Virginia manufacturing facility, I developed a variety of workplace safety initiatives and conducted training on key safety issues for over 1,800 employees. Through my academic background and professional experience, I am well prepared to take on the responsibilities of Director of Plant Safety.

If after reviewing my resume you would like additional information, please contact me. I will be available for an interview at your convenience.

Thank you for considering my application.

Sincerely,

Charles Wilson

PROFESSIONAL/MANAGEMENT INTERNATIONAL MARKETING

WINSTON BURETTE

2186 Pound Street • Atlanta, GA 30339 • (404) 555-8812 (cell) • wburdette@xxx.net

September 23, 20__

Tom Melendez, President
Quasar Corporation
P.O. Box 7742
Atlanta, GA 30338

Dear Mr. Melendez:

I understand that your company is expanding its operations in Asia. As a recent college graduate with a double major in marketing and Japanese, I am well prepared to deal with various tasks related to international trade. Now that my studies have been successfully completed, I would like to offer my services to your company.

Enclosed is a copy of my resume. You will see that along with my academic preparation, I have substantial marketing experience through part-time employment and an internship in Japan with Anderson Consulting. My work record in these situations has been exemplary, as my references will attest.

If a position opens with your company, please consider me. I would be available for part-time or full-time employment. I will be glad to provide additional information by mail or telephone, or to come for an interview.

Thank you for your consideration.

Sincerely yours,

Winston Burette

PROFESSIONAL/MANAGEMENT ACCOUNT MANAGEMENT

JEFFREY H. CROCKETT
657 Wilson Road
Santa Cruz, CA 95060
831/555-5589
831/555-8906 (cell)
jcrockett@xxx.net

December 12, 20__

Mr. Robert Anderson
Anderson Marketing, Inc.
3835 Lincoln Avenue
Ventura, CA 93001

Dear Mr. Anderson:

Because of the excellent reputation of your firm, I am submitting my resume in application for an account management position. Specifically, I am seeking to better utilize my profit-building skills in account prospecting, acquisition, and management.

In my position with Arty Incentives, I have proven my ability to create highly profitable, personalized relationships with key clientele at hundreds of companies. I've executed complex sales with a strong knowledge of product lines, industry trends, and, of course, the customer's specific needs.

My success thus far is a result of comprehensive research and taking an interactive role in a client's business. This allows me to design and implement customized incentive programs while always keeping a sharp eye on bottom-line results.

I am willing to relocate for the right opportunity and can provide excellent references at your request. I will be contacting you soon to arrange a personal interview. Thank you for your time and consideration.

Sincerely,

Jeffrey H. Crockett
enclosure

PROFESSIONAL/MANAGEMENT EDUCATION/SUBSTITUTE TEACHER

ALICE SHAMINSKI
1145 Marlboro Lane
Dublin, NH 03444-0522
603/555-8976 (cell)
ashaminski@xxx.net

April 18, 20__

Teacher Approval Committee
Carlton Language Academy
Dublin, NH 03445

Dear Committee Members:

I am seeking an appointment as an assigned teacher with Carlton Academy. The enclosed resume outlines my teaching experience with learning disabled students in Rolling Knolls.

As mother of an LD student and two college-bound students, I have proven my ability to work effectively with parents of students at virtually all aptitude levels. My activities have included full production supervision of the Rolling Knolls High School Year Book, and I am very interested in volunteer work with Carlton's proposed After School Program.

Please contact me directly to arrange an interview or for further information. Thank you for your time and consideration.

Sincerely,

Alice Shaminski
encl.

PROFESSIONAL/MANAGEMENT BOILERPLATE LETTER FOR AD RESPONSE

ALFRED E. PLATE
574 EAST HUDSON PLACE   CHICAGO, IL 60610
312/555-9276   312/555-8745 (CELL)

July 24, 20__

Mr. Edward Smith
Director of Product Development
Monroe Corporation
598 East Illinois
Chicago, IL 60611

Dear Mr. Smith:

The position of [position name] advertised in last Sunday's [newspaper name] seems tailor made for my qualifications. My experience with [last or current employer] involved responsibility for [several duties listed in the ad], and my efforts resulted in a 20 percent reduction in overhead for 2002. The enclosed resume outlines my qualifications and accomplishments.

I now seek to better utilize my [supervisory/design/organizational, etc.] skills with an industry leader such as [company name, if applicable]. I am willing to travel or relocate, and my salary requirements are negotiable. [You may omit "negotiable" and give a range, such as "upper $50s per year" if requested in the ad.]

I will contact you soon to arrange an interview. Meanwhile, please feel free to give me a call should you require any further information on my background.

Sincerely,

Alfred E. Plate
enclosure

SPECIAL SITUATIONS

The following letters are especially important for people in unusual situations. Here is your chance to explain your circumstances and put them in the best possible light. As mentioned earlier, remember to research the company on the World Wide Web or at your local library, or call the firm directly. If possible, get the name and address of the person in charge of actually hiring for the position at hand—not just the human resources representative.

Like any other cover letter, emphasize your most positive attributes relative to the job. Of course, special product or industry knowledge is preferred, but if you lack this background, try writing about your self-motivation, determination, organizational skills, and/or ability to work independently or as part of a team.

If you're a reliable worker who's also a fast learner, be sure to mention this. A cover letter is a great place to sell your valuable, personal attributes, whether or not you've done them on a job. Of course, try to present these as applicable to a business operation, and you'll be far ahead of applicants who send no letter at all or only a very general cover letter.

TIPS FOR PEOPLE WITH DISABILITIES

There is no consensus on whether a disability should be mentioned in a cover letter. Some feel it should be mentioned if—and only if—it has a direct bearing on the performance of a particular job. On the other hand, keep in mind that some companies may be looking to hire disabled people; if your disability is the type that will have absolutely no bearing on the performance of the job, you may wish to use one sentence of your letter to explain your situation. Again, this should be considered on a job-by-job basis. Overall, here are some key points to consider:

1. You should always stress your ability to do the job, not the existence of a disability.

2. As with any cover letter, it should be addressed to an individual. Also, through your knowledge of the hiring organization, the letter should emphasize how you are the right person for this particular job. Research the company as much as you can prior to writing your letter/resume, even before calling the company to discuss job possibilities.

3. If you think the position might require special adaptive devices, check with the Job Accommodation Network (800-526-7234), a free consulting service that provides information about job accom-

modations, the Americans with Disabilities Act (ADA), and the employability of people with disabilities. If you can determine which devices are available for your situation and that particular type of work, you may be better prepared to answer special questions that may arise at the interview.

4. The Americans with Disabilities Act does not guarantee you a job, just the chance to compete equally. Your resume describes your past accomplishments and activities. The cover letter must get the reader's attention by focusing on special attributes, skills, and knowledge that make you uniquely qualified for the specific job at hand. Avoid repeating items in your resume; just highlight your special qualities that connect you with the job.

5. Each job requires a slightly different letter. Avoid trying to write one that will fit all possibilities.

6. Sit back and take a look at your letter when you finish, and have someone else read it too. Put yourself in the shoes of the interviewer. Would you hire this person? If so, why? Stress the key points in the interview. If you wouldn't hire yourself, write your letter again until your interest and competency show clearly.

COVER LETTER STRATEGIES FOR FORMER PRISON INMATES

Former prison inmates need to take a special approach to job hunting. The example that follows is tailored to meet the concerns of a job seeker whose special circumstances require an approach that goes beyond classified ads and takes a proactive, highly focused approach to the job market.

Using the Internet along with standard local and national business directories, the ex-offender in the example has built a targeted list of publishers who deal with legal materials and desktop publishing, where his skills honed as a prison inmate would be well utilized. The letter is targeted to a specific hiring manager, and it closes by noting that there will be a follow-up call placed to the employer.

Even if the applicant is told when he calls to follow up that there are no openings at that firm, this strategy allows the applicant an entry point for further follow-up. Instead of hanging up and feeling rejected, the letter writer can ask, "Could you suggest a colleague whom I could call at another company that might need my expertise? May I mention to him that I spoke to you?" Managers in a targeted industry generally know other managers and employment trends in the field and can become referral sources for qualified applicants using innovative job search strategies.

SPECIAL SITUATION **FORMER PRISON INMATE**

Terry Berman
1426 Ferry Boulevard • Cleveland, OH 44106
216/555-6788 • tberman@xxx.net

January 17, 20__

Angelo Sorrento
Vice President of Client Services
Baldwin-Corona Publishers
1831 Longfellow Drive
Cleveland, OH 44108

Dear Mr. Sorrento:

As a senior paralegal with eight years of expertise in legal research, desktop publishing, and the editing of technical writing, I believe I can be of benefit to your organization. I am writing to you concerning a position as researcher or writer with your company.

In my previous position, my most significant accomplishments include:
- Conducting paralegal research and court preparation for 20 cases involving prisoners' rights for Appellate Court presentation.
- Writing, researching, and editing a quarterly newsletter circulated by subscription to 2,200 inmates of a maximum security prison.
- Conducting classes on desktop publishing and legal research utilizing LEXIS, WESTLAW, and computerized databases for a seven-member legal research staff.

My previous employer was the Bureau of Prisons, State of Ohio, Lucasville Prison Library. During my incarceration, I received extensive training in desktop publishing and legal research, including earning my B.A. in Paralegal Studies from the University of Dayton extension program.

I have enclosed a resume for your review outlining my background in greater detail. I look forward to meeting with you to discuss the contribution I could make in your setting and will call you within the next two weeks to arrange a mutually agreeable time for an interview.

Sincerely,

Terry Berman
enclosure

SPECIAL SITUATION   RETIREE RETURNING TO WORKFORCE

Steven M. Lasso
220A Woodland Drive
Greenville, OH 45331
937/555-0167
937/666-3443 (cell)

October 4, 20__

Postmaster
United States Post Office
Greenville, OH 45331

Dear Postmaster:

I am exploring the possibility of reinstatement with the U.S. Post Office.

My employment with the USPS overlapped with other employment, during which time it was necessary to hold two positions for financial reasons. I regret this because I truly enjoyed and was proud of my work with the USPS.

In June of this year, I will accept retirement after 26 years of service with EBM and would like to discuss the possibility of joining your post office.

When reviewing my previous work record, please consider my excellent performance and loyalty. I now live in Greenville and would appreciate the chance to give excellent service to my community.

Thank you for your time and consideration, and I look forward to your response.

Yours,

Steven M. Lasso
enclosure

SPECIAL SITUATION EMPLOYMENT AGENCY/SERVICE

MARTIN D. JONES

301 Lexington Lane

Florence, OR 97439

541/555-2103

541/555-2448 (cell)

martin_jones@xxx.net

March 16, 20__

Mr. Ed Bruno
The Edison Group
433 Third Avenue
Seattle, WA 98119

Dear Mr. Bruno:

I am exploring opportunities in sales and/or sales management and would like to work with your firm. Specifically, I am seeking to better utilize my talents in sales team building, staff training, and motivation.

My creativity and profit-building skills, developed primarily with Crenshaw Corporation, have resulted in increased market share and reduced staff turnover. My high-energy approach to business development, tempered with personalized account servicing, produces satisfied clients and repeat business. This is the type of success I am certain I can now duplicate with any company.

I can provide excellent references upon request and am willing to travel for the right opportunity. Please let me know as soon as possible when we can meet for an interview and discuss mutual interests. I look forward to your response.

Thank you for your time and consideration.

Sincerely,

Martin D. Jones
enclosure

SPECIAL SITUATION VETERAN RETURNING TO WORK

JAMES A. BURKE
75 Berwick Place
Tucker, GA 30085
770/555-9545
770/555-3202 (cell)

February 21, 20__

Dear Hiring Manager:

My experience includes direct responsibility for staff education as well as super-vision of a wide range of operations. My work with the U.S. Marines has made me highly self-motivated and disciplined, and I've successfully trained and motivated others in both communications and daily operations:

- I've proven my ability to work effectively with leaders and work crews at all levels of experience.
- My solid record of achievement was gained both by coordinating staff and tackling a wide range of projects, not only with efficiency, but with a sharp eye on detail and quality.

I can provide excellent references upon request, including letters of commen-dation. Please let me know as soon as possible when we may meet for an inter-view and discuss mutual interests. I look forward to your response.

Thank you for your time and consideration.

Sincerely,

James A. Burke
enclosure

SPECIAL SITUATION   BASIC LETTER, SPANISH-SPEAKING APPLICANT

JOSE GARCIA
4362 Bell Avenue
Sacramento, CA 95814
(906) 555-3448

June 19, 20__

Ms. Mary L. Henderson
455 West Hall Road
Sacramento, CA 95814

Muy estimada Ms. Henderson:

He leído con gran interés el anuncio que Uds. publicaron en e *Sacramento Bee* el 16 de enero de 2003, en el cual solicitan un administrador de oficina. Con el fin de considerarme candidato al Puesto, le acliunto mi currículum vitae.

Por los detalles contenidos en el mismo, pueden demostrar que reuno las califi-caciones para desempeñar a su satisfacción el puesto que tienen vacante. Desde hace cinco años trabajo en la oficina central de California Fidelity Bank, donde entré como cajero y, a través de asceusos, desempeño en la actualidad el cargo de administrador de oficina. Por lo tanto, estoy familia rizado con todas las respon-sibilidades de la oficina.

Espero que me concedan una entrevista a su más pronta conveniencia.

Atentamente,

José Garciá

English Translation

Dear Ms. Henderson:

I have read with interest your ad in the *Sacramento Bee* (January 16, 2003) seeking an office administrator. I am pleased to enclose a copy of my resume so that I might be considered as a candidate for the position.

The details of my resume demonstrate that I am qualified to fill the vacant position. For the past five years, I have been working in the main office of California Fidelity Bank; I started as a cashier, and, through promotions, I am now Office Administrator. I am, therefore, knowledgeable about all office functions.

I hope you will grant me an interview at your earliest convenience.

Sincerely,

Jose Garcia

SPECIAL SITUATION BASIC LETTER, SPANISH-SPEAKING APPLICANT

JUAN HERNANDEZ
2320 Greenview Terrace
Aspen, CO 81611
970/555-6678
970/555-2268 (cell)

Mr. Leon Jackson
Environmental Consortium, Ltd.
345 Westcott Place
Prairie Village, KS 66208

Muy estimado, Mr. Jackson:

Me dirijo a usted con el fin de explorar posibilidades de empleo con su dinámica compania. Por consiguiente, le ajunto, mi curriculum vitae.

Los detalles de mi experiencia profesional hacen constatar que tengo grandes conocimientos en el campo de productos para la limpieza biodegradables. Durante los últimos trés aflos he sido gerente para un fabricante de productos similares. Me interesa, sobre todo, un puesto en el cual podria desarollar productos nuevos e innovadores.

Espero que me concedan una entrevista a su más pronta conveniencia.

Atentamente,

Juan Hernandez

English Translation

Dear Mr. Jackson:

I am writing to you in order to explore employment opportunities with your dynamic organization. Accordingly, I have enclosed a copy of my resume.

The details of my resume attest that I have experience in the field of biodegradable cleaning products. For the past three years, I have been a manager for a manufacturer of a similar line. I am especially interested in a position that would allow me to develop new and innovative products.

I hope you will grant me an interview at your earliest convenience.

Sincerely,

Juan Hernandez

SPECIAL SITUATION HOUSEWIFE RETURNING TO THE WORKFORCE

Joan Jackson

258 Old Farm Road   Columbus, OH 43215

614/555-0961   jmjackson@xxx.net

September 10, 20___

Personnel Department
P.O. Box 4325
Columbus, OH 43215

Dear Personnel Representative:

With my wide range of skills developed in various community groups and as a homemaker, your advertisement for Assistant Store Supervisor in Sunday's *Columbus Dispatch* seems written with my qualifications in mind.

In addition to the information on my enclosed resume, I have greatly expanded my skills in time and money management, workflow scheduling, and project coordination. These are just a few of the skills required to run a busy home with four children, all of whom are now in college or pursuing their own successful careers.

As my resume indicates, I have been very active as a volunteer docent at our community library and have served as president of the School Parent/Teacher Association. I've also been active in fund-raising for various programs, and my communication and motivational skills resulted in over $29,000 in cash donations to our library and the TWIGS Christmas Bazaar.

Because this letter and resume only summarize my full qualifications, I would welcome the chance to meet with you personally to discuss your particular business needs. To that end, I look forward to hearing from you soon.

Thank you for your prompt consideration.

Sincerely,

Joan Jackson
enclosure

ADDITIONAL COVER LETTER FRAGMENTS

The following paragraphs are taken from cover letters expressing interest in a variety of positions. For the sake of simplicity, these examples omit addresses, inside addresses, and other traditional elements of business letters (see previous samples for full versions of such letters). Instead, the following examples are offered to provide ideas for wording to use and points to make in the main body of your cover letters.

APPROACH: FOLLOW-UP TO TELEPHONE CONVERSATION

Emphasis: Similarity of related experience

Thank you for talking with me this morning. I enjoyed our telephone conversation. As you requested, I am enclosing a copy of my resume. This will provide you with specific details regarding my experience, training, and overall qualifications.

You will note that I have a great deal of experience in project management, from developing initial plans to completing final reports. My background with Thompson Consulting has prepared me to work with a wide range of engineering projects. Over the past four years I have proven to be reliable, conscientious, and innovative in serving client needs and seeing projects through to successful completion.

APPROACH: INTRODUCTION BASED ON PERSONAL REFERRAL

Emphasis: Similarity of related experience

I would like to apply for the position of Executive Secretary in your company's public relations office in Memphis. Mr. Brian Fox, my former supervisor and a current member of the public relations staff at your Dothan, Alabama, offices, informed me of this opening and suggested that I apply.

A copy of my resume is enclosed. As you will see, I have had substantial secretarial experience in a public relations setting. In addition, my technical skills include a rated word-processing speed of 90 words per minute and mastery of a variety of desktop publishing software packages.

APPROACH: INTRODUCTION

Emphases: (1) Relocation and (2) Specific qualifications

As a qualified radiologic laboratory technician who will soon be relocating to the Cleveland area, I would like to apply for any open position you may have for technicians.

A copy of my resume is enclosed. As you will note, I have four years of experience in the field and can demonstrate appropriate educational credentials as well as national certification.

APPROACH: FOLLOW-UP TO WEB POSTING

Emphasis: Similarity of related experience

I noted in reviewing your college's website that you plan to hire a fiscal technician. I would like to apply for this position (job number 33F).

A copy of my resume is enclosed. You will see that I possess all the necessary skills and training for this position. In addition, my previous experience at Westfield State College has prepared me well to function with a diverse group of staff, faculty, and students.

APPROACH: INTRODUCTION BASED ON PERSONAL REFERRAL

Emphasis: Academic background

I understand from our mutual acquaintance, Jason Ramirez, that you may have an opening soon in your public relations department. If so, I would be highly interested in applying.

I recently received a bachelor's degree from McGill University with a double major in marketing and public relations. This educational background was supplemented by summer work experience in public relations for a major publishing company in Montreal.

A copy of my resume is enclosed. As you will see, I have taken a variety of challenging courses and have been an outstanding student. If you would like writing samples or other information, please let me know.

APPROACH: RESPONSE TO WEBSITE POSTING

Emphases: (1) Similarity of related experience and (2) Availability of work samples

This is to apply for the graphic designer position that has recently become open at your company, as noted on your corporate website.

Please see the enclosed resume for an overview of my educational background and work experience. The latter included two years at Wilson Advertising in Santa Fe, where I produced a variety of graphic materials and played a substantial experience role in web page design. As I understand it, this is very similar to the expectations for the position you have advertised.

Would you like to review samples of my work? If so, please let me know. I will be happy to send samples via E-mail, to mail photocopies, or to bring a portfolio for your inspection. Of course, I am available for an interview at your convenience.

APPROACH: RESPONSE TO NEWSPAPER ADVERTISEMENT

Emphasis: Similarity of related experience

I was excited to see the advertisement in the *Greenville News* that the Greenville County School System is seeking an interpreter for the deaf. Please accept this letter and the enclosed resume as my application for the position.

Upon reviewing my resume, you will see that I have the appropriate training and certifications for this position. In addition, my previous public school experiences have prepared me for further success in educational interpreting. I would enjoy the opportunity to contribute to student success while working in such an environment.

APPROACH: RESPONSE TO A NEWSLETTER ANNOUNCEMENT

Emphasis: Academic background

As a recent college graduate with a background in the fine arts, I would like to apply for the position of Assistant Curator as recently announced in the *Metro Arts Scene* newsletter.

The enclosed resume details my education and experience. As you will see, my studies at the University of Kentucky focused on art history and arts management. I have worked in the South Lexington Fine Arts Center the past two summers, performing duties very similar to those listed in your job announcement. I also have experience in coordinating art outreach programs for children as well as adults.

APPROACH: "COLD" (UNSOLICITED) INTRODUCTION WITHOUT IDENTIFIED JOB OPENING

Emphasis: Academic background

In the event that you have any openings for new project engineers, I am submitting the enclosed resume for your review.

As you will see, I have proven experience in designing and testing biotechnology equipment through my recent internship at Iowa State University. I worked under the supervision of Dr. Pamela Cremmons, a frequent consultant for your company. I am sure Dr. Cremmons can vouch for my technical capabilities as well as my strong work ethic and positive attitude.

APPROACH: "COLD" (UNSOLICITED) INTRODUCTION BASED ON PROJECTED JOB OPENING

Emphases: (1) Appropriate experience and (2) Academic background

I understand from recent publicity that the city's recreation department may be expanding in the near future. As new positions become available, I would appreciate the opportunity to apply.

A copy of my resume is enclosed. As you will see, I have more than three years of direct experience in athletic administration. I also hold a bachelor's degree in recreation management from Kansas State University.

In addition, my recent experience as a professional basketball player in Europe has widened my horizons. Although my playing career ended after one year, I learned a great deal about teamwork, a positive attitude, and the logistical side of sports and recreation.

APPROACH: RESPONSE TO A NEWSPAPER ADVERTISEMENT

Emphasis: Direct skills complemented by academic background

This is to apply for one of the two position openings you have recently advertised in the *Washington Post* for computer repair technicians. As requested in your ad, I am enclosing a resume that includes the names and phone numbers of three references.

I have three solid years of experience as a computer repair technician for a large government agency. I also have earned 36 credits toward an associate's degree in Information Systems Technology at Northern Virginia Community College. You will find me a task-oriented, thorough worker with outstanding troubleshooting skills.

APPROACH: RESPONSE TO A NEWSPAPER ADVERTISEMENT

Emphases: (1) Direct skills and (2) Aftermath of plant closing

I would like to apply for the assembly line position advertised by your company in Sunday's *Des Moines Register*. A copy of my resume is enclosed.

As you will see, I have had previous manufacturing experience. I received very positive evaluations during my time at Poly-Tech Manufacturing until its closing last month. In fact, I was named Employee of the Month just last June.

I feel that my experience should provide a strong match with the duties of your position. Please see my resume for more details.

APPROACH: FOLLOW-UP TO TELEPHONE CONVERSATION

Emphases: (1) Appropriate related experience and (2) Positive work performance

Thank you for talking with me this afternoon. I enjoyed our telephone conversation and appreciated the information you provided.

As outlined on my resume, I have had five years of experience in maintaining refrigeration systems. I am familiar with the appropriate equipment and am a dependable worker with an excellent work ethic and a record of positive performance evaluations.

APPROACH: FOLLOW-UP TO NEWSPAPER ADVERTISEMENT

Emphases: (1) Similarity of related experience and (2) Relevant special interest

The enclosed resume is submitted in application for the position of Marketing Coordinator for your organization as advertised in the Daily Beacon.

My solid background in marketing provides a good match for the duties required of this position. While employed with another not-for-profit organization, I specialized in performing duties quite similar to those listed in your job announcement.

In addition to my professional background, I have long been interested in history and have served in several leadership capacities with volunteer organizations related to historic preservation. I would enjoy being associated with an organization such as yours with an obvious commitment to conserving this country's historical treasures.

APPROACH: "COLD" (UNSOLICITED) CONTACT

Emphasis: Directly related experience and skills

I understand that your company operates a substantial auto maintenance and repair operation to support the large number of vehicles used by your sales and delivery personnel. I'm an experienced mechanic with up-to-date skills in all aspects of automotive repair and as such would like to offer my services should a position become available.

A copy of my resume is enclosed. You will see that I have over seven years of experience in the field, most recently at Wilson Motors, where I received excellent evaluations from my superiors. I have also completed a variety of classes and seminars on various automotive topics (see complete list provided).

APPROACH: RESPONSE TO NEWSPAPER ADVERTISEMENT

Emphasis: Similarity of related experience

Please accept the enclosed resume in application for the position of maintenance director at your organization. This is in response to the job vacancy notice published this week in the *Herald-Dispatch*.

As you will gather from my resume, I have solid experience in supervising maintenance and custodial services. In fact, I believe that my professional background provides the ideal qualifications you are seeking.

APPROACH: FOLLOW-UP TO IN-PERSON CONVERSATION

Emphasis: Similarity of related experience

Thank you for talking with me yesterday. I am glad we ran into one another. As you requested, I am enclosing a copy of my resume. This will provide you with specific details regarding my background and qualifications.

As you will see, I have a great deal of experience in developing surveys and other research materials. For example, I designed a series of customer satisfaction surveys for major retailers, including CVS Pharmacies and JC Penney. These experiences, along with the appropriate academic preparation, have prepared me to handle the kind of tasks you mentioned in our conversation.

APPROACH: RESPONSE TO WEBSITE POSTING

Emphases: (1) Directly related experience and (2) Demonstrated record of success

I was interested to see on your corporate website that your company is looking for new sales associates. Please accept the enclosed resume as my application for a position in this area.

As you will note, my background and experience provide a close match with the requirements described in your position announcement. I am a proven self-starter with highly developed skills in setting goals and meeting them. My communication skills are excellent, and I have earned several awards for successful sales performance (see resume for complete listing).

APPROACH: RESPONSE TO NEWSPAPER ADVERTISEMENT

Emphasis: Similarity of related experience

I would like to apply for the position of financial support specialist as advertised in Sunday's edition of the *Post-Gazette*. Enclosed are a resume and the names of three references as stipulated in the job announcement.

As noted in my resume, I have a solid track record in maintaining financial records. This includes four years of experience as a fiscal technician at Webber Telecommunications and another two years at my current position with the American Red Cross.

APPROACH: "COLD" (UNSOLICITED) CONTACT REGARDING POSSIBLE OPENINGS

Emphasis: Academic background

Enclosed is my resume for your consideration for any suitable openings in your operations in Illinois, Indiana, or Ohio. I would be interested in applying for any such positions that may become open in the near future. I believe that my training and strong work ethic will allow me to make a significant contribution to your company.

I am currently completing a bachelor's degree in marketing at Indiana State University. Although I am currently enrolled as a full-time student, I am available for employment immediately following completion of the current semester. I am also willing to relocate.

APPROACH: RESPONSE TO WEBSITE POSTING

Emphases: (1) Similarity of related experience and (2) Availability of work samples

Please accept this letter and the enclosed resume in application for the position of staff writer announced on your website.

My extensive background in writing newspaper articles and advertising copy provides a good match for the requirements described in your job announcement. I have three years of experience in writing for a weekly newspaper and have experienced in developing a wide range of advertising copy, including print ads, radio and television commercials, annual reports, and web copy. I'm confident I could help meet your demand for well-written material.

Please review my resume and let me know if you feel my background fits with the needs of your company. I'll be glad to provide a portfolio of my work or to tackle a sample assignment to demonstrate my ability to work quickly and accurately.

APPROACH: FOLLOW-UP TO PHONE CONVERSATION

Emphasis: Similarity of related experience

Thank you for taking the time to talk with me yesterday about employment possibilities with your company. Your enthusiasm about Winslow Enterprises seems contagious, for I am highly interested in following up on our conversation.

A copy of my resume is enclosed for your review. You will note, as we discussed, that I have had three years of successful experience as a customer service specialist. I am a hard worker who enjoys working with the public. I have excellent communication skills as well as strong organizational capabilities.

APPROACH: "COLD" (UNSOLICITED) CONTACT

Emphasis: Similarity of related experience in current job

I am writing to express my interest in obtaining a position with your bank. I am familiar with your organization as a customer and have always been impressed with your operations.

A copy of my resume is enclosed. As you will see, I am an experienced employee with another successful financial services firm. Along with holding excellent educational credentials, I am skilled in providing an array of support services for customers.

APPROACH: FOLLOW-UP TO PERSONAL CONVERSATION

Emphases: (1) Academic background and (2) Part-time job experience

As you may recall, I spoke with you last year regarding possible employment with your firm following completion of my studies at Clemson University. Now that my degree is in hand, I would like to express interest in employment.

A copy of my resume is enclosed for your review. As you will note, in addition to my bachelor's degree in public relations, I have had considerable work experience through internships and part-time employment in the public relations field. It is my hope to build upon this background by working in a leading organization such as yours.

APPROACH: FOLLOW-UP TO TELEPHONE CONVERSATION

Emphasis: Personal traits related to job

Thanks for taking the time to speak with me this afternoon. As one who is eager to advance my career in sales and marketing, I am submitting the enclosed resume for your review. I would appreciate being considered as an addition to your staff.

To amplify on our conversation, my background includes two successful positions in outside sales (see resume for more details). In both of these roles, I gained invaluable background in self-motivation, time management, communication skills, and other attributes vital to successful sales performance.

I am a diligent worker who enjoys learning new skills and techniques. My positive attitude and emphasis on teamwork would be valuable assets for your organization.

APPROACH: "COLD" (UNSOLICITED) SUBMISSION BASED ON COMPANY PROFILE

Emphasis: Academic background with specialized training

I understand that your firm employs a number of computer repair technicians. I have recently completed an associate's degree in computer technology at Trident Technical College, where I acquired a variety of maintenance and repair skills. Now that my studies have concluded, I am eager to apply my capabilities in the workplace.

Enclosed is a copy of my resume. As you will see, I have training in a broad range of tasks needed for working with computers and related equipment. In fact, I completed 12 additional credits beyond degree requirements to acquire the broadest possible capabilities. I can offer excellent work habits, outstanding technical capabilities, and a thorough, dedicated approach to work.

APPROACH: "COLD" (UNSOLICITED) CONTACT BASED ON PLANNED RELOCATION

Emphasis: Related experience

This is to inquire about possible employment with your company. I am planning to relocate to the St. Louis area next month and would be very interested in joining your staff should a position become available.

My background in the drafting field includes three years of experience with Compass Engineering here in Louisville, where I have performed a wide range of drafting and design services. This has included operating the latest computer equipment and CAD software.

APPROACH: LOW-KEY RESPONSE TO THIRD-PARTY CONTACT

Emphases: (1) Academic background and (2) Desire for career change

Meredith Carter showed me your company's annual report and suggested I contact you. Your firm's accomplishments are most impressive.

A copy of my resume is enclosed for your review should you desire to expand your staff in line with recent growth. As you can see, I have had a highly successful career as a manager for not-for-profit organizations. I would now like to apply the leadership and communication skills developed over the past fourteen years to the financial services arena. I have been preparing for this career change for some time and this year completed a master's degree in finance with a specialty in investment management.

I believe that my skills and training would be an asset to your company as you position your organization in an increasingly competitive market. My skills should be particularly useful in your efforts to market financial products to those in the not-for-profit sector.

FOLLOW-UP LETTERS

It is an excellent idea to send a follow-up letter after mailing a resume or completing an interview at a company. Many applicants fail to do this. But when you send a letter, you show the company that you're very self-motivated and interested in the job.

To follow up on a resume you've sent a company, you should state that you recently sent a resume to the company and name the position. Tell the reader you are still very interested in the job and that you would like to meet with the hiring authority for a personal interview. Here you can also restate key talents and skills that make you uniquely qualified for the job. Wait about one week after sending your resume before sending this letter.

A simple interview follow-up letter begins by thanking the reader for the interview and discussing important aspects of the job and your abilities. It ends by thanking the reader again for the interview and restating your interest in working for such a great company. You should send this letter within one or two days of your interview.

FOLLOW-UP RESUME SENT

KENNETH P. HONDA
142 Dorchester Court
Providence, RI 02903
401/555-8888
401/555-4312 (cell)

November 6, 20__

Dear Hiring Manager:

I recently sent you a resume and cover letter in application for the position of Sales Representative. This letter is to confirm your receipt of my resume, as well as my very strong interest in your company.

My successful, hands-on experience and education would prove highly valuable to your operation. However, my resume and cover letter can only provide a brief explanation of my background, and I would therefore like the chance to meet with you personally to discuss your particular business needs. To that end, I look forward to hearing from you soon.

Thanks again for your time and consideration.

Sincerely,

Kenneth P. Honda

DEBRA ROBERTS

897 Salem Trail #B2
Harrisburg, PA 17105-2955
727/555-1265

February 7, 20__

Jane Alvin
Regional Sales Manager
Compaq Corporation
P.O. Box 1277
Philadelphia, PA 19103

Dear Ms. Alvin,

Thank you for your time and for a very informative interview on Monday. It was a pleasure meeting you, and I was most impressed by the high professional standards demonstrated by your staff.

I am certain my sales and marketing skills would prove extremely valuable as a member of your Mid-Atlantic Regional Sales Team. Your product line is excellent, and your company has proven its ability to reach both new and expanding markets.

Once again, thank you for your consideration. I look forward to new career challenges with your excellent firm.

Sincerely,

Debra Roberts

FOLLOW-UP INTERVIEW/EXECUTIVE LEVEL

RALPH D. STEPHAN
334 Crestview Drive • Royal Oak, MI 48067
248/555-3532 • ralphman@usit.net

September 30, 20___

Mr. Roger J. Krause
Liquid Container Company
275 Nuclear Drive
Chicago, IL 60611

Dear Roger:

Thank you for a very interesting and informative interview regarding the position at Liquid Container. If I monopolized the conversation, it was due simply to the excitement and enthusiasm I was feeling based on knowing I am the correct fit for the position.

As we discussed, I do feel that a restructure of the sales commission/bonus plans with a keen eye to immediacy of reward, skewed substantially toward repeat and add-on business, would be beneficial.

I also feel that intensive field support, combined with a program to establish ongoing interaction with key account decision makers, would clearly identify the new role and authority of your sales staff. This would also serve to solidify your manager's commitment to relationship-building opportunities for all accounts.

I feel my prior experience in full-spectrum manufacturing of household and auto after-market chemicals gives me an in-depth knowledge of potential customer needs, from packaging to desired consumer benefits. To put it quite simply, I know what customers want because I was previously in their position.

Through my conversation with you, I feel that the position provides exactly the type of long-term career opportunity I am seeking. I am fully confident that I will prove to be a valuable asset to you and your division, and look forward to meeting with you again to further discuss your needs and my qualifications.

Yours truly,

Ralph D. Stefan

REFERENCE AND SALARY HISTORY SHEETS

It is always a good idea to have reference and salary history sheets printed in case they're requested by an employer. Many advertisements now ask that you send one or both of these sheets with your resume. Salary history sheets are especially valuable to employers who are looking for an applicant at a certain salary level. Bring copies of each of these to your interviews, in case they're requested by the employer. Always be prepared!

Follow the examples below for both of these sheets, but remember not to send them unless requested by the employer. This is especially true of salary history sheets, because you may come across as over- or underpriced for the position. If you are willing to work at a lower pay scale, you should add: "Current salary requirements are open to negotiation."

If an employer requests only salary requirements, don't send a salary history at all, but instead give them a salary range in your cover letter such as: "I am currently seeking a position in the range of $30,000-$35,000 per year."

When listing references, separate them into business and personal, and try to have three to five of each. Be sure to call your references first and make sure it's okay if you use their names.

SAMPLE REFERENCE SHEET

JOHN H. DOAN, JR.
References

Business

Bruce Gin, President
Fairfield Marine, Inc.
5739 Dixie Highway
Columbus, OH 43215
614/555-0825
www.fmi.com

Brian Krixen, Partner
Ernst & Young
150 South Wacker Drive
Chicago, IL 60606
312/555-1800
bkrixen@eandy.com

Jay Cook, VP Sales/Marketing
Jayco Inc.
P.O. Box 460
Indianapolis, IN 46204
317/555-5861
jc2@jayco.com

Jim E. Shields, President
Shields Southwest Sales, Inc.
1008 Brady Avenue NW
Atlanta, GA 30309
404/555-1133

Personal

Richard Baeson, Yamaha
Business Development Manager
P.O. Box 8234
Evansville, IN 47715
812/555-8846
richardb@yahamain.com

Bob Redson, Salesman
Central Photo Engraving
712 South Prairie Avenue
Chicago, IL 60616
708/555-9119
708/555-3884 (cell)

Dan Linder, CPA
Conklin Accounting & Tax Service
5262 South Rt. 83 #308
Indianapolis, IN 46206
317/555-9004
317/555-4722 (cell)

Baden Powell, Manager
Smith Leasing Corporation
4454 Cookview Road
Athens, GA 30603
706/555-6353

SAMPLE SALARY HISTORY

STEVEN A. ROGERS
Salary History
(Annual Basis)

People Search, Inc.
Human Resources Representative: $45,000

Anderson Employment, Inc.
Staff Writer: up to $35,000 (commission-based)

National Van Lines
Corporate Recruiter: $30,000

Professional Career Consultants
Writer and Branch Manager: up to $30,000 (commission-based)

Notes:

- You could also add: "Salary requirements are open to negotiation."

- If salary requirements are requested, you could write: "Currently seeking a position in the high $40s (or low $50s, etc.) per year."

- Remember that the figures you report could label you as overpriced or underpriced for the position. That's one reason employers ask for a salary history in the first place.

- Also remember that unless the employer requests, do not include salary history or requirements.

Printing and Distributing Your Cover Letter and Resume

Cover letters and resumes are most commonly used to respond to advertisements or to apply for specific, open positions within a company. However, this represents only a fraction of the uses you can put to them. With all of the time and effort you've invested in crafting your documents, it's only right to make use of them by distributing them to appropriate persons and at appropriate times. This section explores the various additional uses as well as some tips for mailing and following up on your submissions.

WHERE TO USE

NETWORKING

The best, if perhaps least common, use of a resume is in networking. If you're out of work, make sure those people you know in the industry have a copy of your resume. Give copies to your family and friends, or anyone at all who might know a company president, manager, supervisor, or influential professional in your field. Acquaintances from professional groups and associations also can be valuable.

On the other hand, if you are still employed and must maintain confidentiality, offer your resume only to people you can really trust. Ask that they refrain from informing your boss or others at your company about your intention to leave.

EMPLOYMENT AGENCIES

Don't underestimate the power of a private employment agency or your state's job service offices. They often have positions that are not advertised because of the client firm's desire for confidentiality or detachment from the screening process. Be sure to register with the more established firms and avoid any sleazy operations that make promises they can't keep. Avoid paying resume-writing and clerical charges disguised as "out-of-pocket expenses." Unless you really believe the agency can help you out, let the employer pay the fees. In general, never pay for a job.

COLD CALLING

Drop in off the street, in business attire of course, and fill out applications at businesses or not-for-profit organizations in your area. Try to research these companies first and leave a resume with your application. Call the hiring authority the next day to follow up. Even when providing a resume, never refuse to complete a job application, and avoid writing "see resume" instead of valuable information. Completing the job application is your first assignment with the company, so do it!

DIFFERENT TYPES OF ADVERTISEMENTS

Blind box ads are used by companies that don't want to be identified, and they pay extra for the privilege. This keeps their own employees from learning about the position and lets them maintain confidentiality. This type of ad also relieves the firm of maintaining its public image by sending the ubiquitous rejection letter. Respond to blind ads if the position seems right for you, but don't expect much. You can't call or research the company, you don't know where it's located, and you can't personalize a cover letter. Don't forget advertisements in trade journals and magazines related to your field. By the way, the company placing the blind ad could be your own!

Many job openings are now posted on Internet sites. One way to find such announcements is to use any search engine and enter the term "jobs" followed by the field in which you are interested. You can then peruse the sites identified. Several large commercial sites offer hundreds of job listings on any given day. In addition, you may find smaller or more specialized sites to be valuable.

Many companies and non-profit organizations also post job openings on their own websites. Simply access the home page and then look for headings such as "jobs," "employment," or "human resources." You can then review announcements of job vacancies and, if appropriate, submit your resume and cover letter.

COLLEGE CAREER CENTERS

Career centers or career services offices at colleges and universities (formerly known as placement offices) can be very helpful sources of information and assistance. Whether you're a student or a graduate, such a center is worth checking out to obtain information about job openings or help with the job search process. In some cases, you can obtain help (or at least access to books, videos, career interest tests, or other information) from a local college even if you never attended there.

CAREER/JOB FAIRS

Career and job fairs are great places to drop off resumes with many companies and save time, travel, and postage (a cover letter may not be expected). These fairs offer the chance to have mini-interviews right on the spot. There are free job fairs at colleges and hotels listed in many Sunday newspapers and on websites. Begin with the fairs that charge no admission fee and review the list of companies before you attend.

TIPS ON MAILING AND FOLLOW-UP

When possible, use large 9″ × 12″ envelopes to mail your cover letter and resume. This costs a bit more, but your correspondence arrives flat and clean. If you're responding to a blind P.O. box ad, use a standard envelope with sufficient postage, but be sure to fold your letter neatly.

Call the company on the date you mail your cover letter and resume, and try to speak directly with the manager or hiring authority. If that's impossible, at least talk to the personnel or human resources representative. Give your name and note that you've sent a resume in application for a position. Try to strike up a conversation about your qualifications and how they're just right for the job, but don't oversell yourself if the person sounds too busy to talk.

Of course, if the advertisement or posting says NO CALLS PLEASE, then don't call—unless you can anonymously learn the hiring authority's name and/or title from the receptionist. In that case, try calling that person directly to inquire about opportunities in your field, as if you've never seen the ad and heard about the company through industry contacts or a friend. Be prepared to handle yourself well if you try this!

Keep a written list, card file, or computer list of resumes sent to whom and on what date. Ideally, you should call the company three to four days after sending your resume and try to speak with the actual hiring authority. Tell this person you want to confirm that he or she has received your resume and that you would like to arrange an interview. Try to speak directly with the manager or supervisor, but if that's impossible, try the personnel representative. However, be sure not to make a pest of yourself. Hounding anyone on the telephone is perceived as pushy and desperate.

An extreme example of this problem occurred with an applicant whom the hiring manager had already interviewed. The manager felt that although the candidate had energy and some degree of experience, it just wasn't the kind of experience essential to this particular job. After learning he had not been hired, the applicant called the manager's office at least 10 times over the next two weeks to tell her more about his background and why he thought the company was the right employer for him. The applicant acutely annoyed the receptionist and only confirmed the manager's suspicions of immaturity.

If the manager or representative refuses to speak with you or set an interview, give it one more try over the next day or two. Then sit tight or send a follow-up letter. Don't be discouraged by being told "we're reviewing the applications and will be arranging interviews as soon as we've screened them all." This is the standard "don't call us, we'll call you" line, and it's not without justification. Sometimes employers really do want to sift through resumes first and then decide whom to meet.

The whole idea of resume follow-up is to drop your name into the mind of the manager or representative and distance yourself from the silent stack of resumes. If you can set an interview, fine. But remember that employers have time constraints and perhaps hundreds of resumes to screen, so don't be dismayed.

MOTIVATION IS ESSENTIAL

When all is said and done, you must stay motivated no matter how long it takes to get interviews. It's the person who stays persistent and positive that who finally gets in the door.

Some people approach their job search with a "me against them" attitude, "them" being the prospective employer. They see only a wall of indifference from hiring managers and personnel representatives. This can be fatal to a job search. As hard as it may seem, you need to project yourself as an ally to all staff and managers at the target organization. Try to act as if you are already part of their operation. Focus on creating a "we" scenario without being presumptuous. Remember, these are people with whom you hope soon to be working.

The Interview

If you manage to get one interview for every 20 resumes sent in response to advertisements, you're doing fairly well. Even if you have several interviews booked, don't stop researching, checking advertisements, and sending resumes. Always hedge yourself in case an interview is canceled. However, don't book too many interviews on the same day. Some may run two to three hours, and you may be late getting to the next one. Never be late for an interview! Leave early and allow for bad weather, traffic jams, or other problems. The single most important thing to remember about the interview is: don't be nervous.

Any decent interviewer understands that you may be nervous, especially if it's one of your very first interviews. Interviewers should know how to put you at ease right from the start with some light conversation, rather than put you on the spot, but don't count on it. Some interviewers actually enjoy intimidating candidates with difficult questions or tricky situations to see how they react under pressure. Just keep in mind that it's all a show to see what you're made of. Keep your composure as much as possible, thoughtfully consider your replies, and maintain eye contact with the interviewer when responding.

An interview is not a life-or-death situation. Relax and just be yourself. Easier said than done? Remember that you're not the only person who will be interviewed for the job. The company may be interviewing other candidates who come across as more relaxed and confident but don't have the skills and experience you have. Don't let them get the job!

No matter how intimidating interviewers may seem, remember that they probably sat right where you are and answered similar questions to get their jobs. In fact, the more relaxed the candidate becomes, the more relaxed interviewers tend to become. The result can be conversations that are more informative and natural.

Get excited about the interview as a discovery process. Be aware of whether you talk too much or too little. At the same time, feel free to ask questions about the company without appearing skeptical. Try to give the interviewer an honest impression of confidence (without being cocky), personality (without being a clown), and intelligence (without talking down to the interviewer).

If you are consistently calm and measured in your answers and the interviewer seems inattentive, overbearing, or gives vague responses to questions about compensation, work hours, or specific job duties, don't waste your time. Forget the company and find a better place to spend 40 to 50 hours of your life every week. Throughout your job search, no matter how hard it seems, you must always keep a positive attitude. Act professionally and courteously—with the receptionist, with everyone. Dress professionally—look the part.

The single most important factor, as with anything in life, is to keep a positive attitude. Maintain eye contact and speak clearly on the phone, at the interview, with the receptionist, with everyone. Remember, these people may soon be your coworkers. Everyone wants to be around a winner, so act like a winner.

Appendix A
Further Reading

Many of the books included below provide sample resumes, cover letters, and other informative material. Others provide tips on the job search process or on other career-related matters.

You can obtain these books at major bookstores or through online book retailers. Or visit your local library and inquire about them. Also, ask your librarian to direct you to reference materials on the specific industry or business you're interested in.

Abel, Alicia. *Business Grammar, Style & Usage: The Desk Reference for Articulate and Polished Business Writing, Speaking & Correspondence.* Aspatore Books, 2003.

Adams, Bob. *The Everything Job Interview Book.* Adams Media Corporation, 2001.

Adams, Bob, and Laura Morin. *The Complete Resume & Job Search Book for College Students.* Adams Media Corporation, 1999.

Allen, Jeffrey G. *The Resume Makeover.* John Wiley and Sons, 2001.

Beatty, Richard H. 175 *High-Impact Cover Letters.* John Wiley and Sons, 2002.

Beatty, Richard H. *The Perfect Cover Letter.* John Wiley and Sons, 1996.

Besson, Tannee S., and *National Business Employment Weekly. Cover Letters.* John Wiley & Sons, 1999.

Besson, Tannee S., and *National Business Employment Weekly. Resumes.* John Wiley & Sons, 1999.

Bloch, Deborah Perlmutter. *How to Get Your First Job and Keep It.* McGraw-Hill, 2002.

Block, Jay. *101 Best Cover Letters*. McGraw-Hill, 1999.

Block, Jay. 101 *Best Resumes to Sell Yourself*. McGraw-Hill, 2002.

Brown, Lola. *Resume Writing Made Easy*. Pearson Education, 2002.

Criscito, Pat. *Designing the Perfect Resume*. Barron's Educational Series, 2000.

Cunningham, John R. *The Inside Scoop: Recruiters Share Their Tips on Job Search Success with College Students*. McGraw-Hill, 2001.

Drake, John D. *The Perfect Interview: How to Get the Job You Really Want*. Fine Publications, 2002.

Enelow, Wendy S., and Louise Kursmark. *Cover Letter Magic*. JIST Works, 2000.

Editors, VGM Career Books. *Resumes for Re-Entering the Job Market*. McGraw-Hill, 2002.

Eisenberg, Ronni. *Organize Your Job Search!* Hyperion Press, 2000.

Farr, J. Michael. *The Quick Resume and Cover Letter Book*. JIST Works, Inc., 2000.

Garber, Janet. *Getting a Job*. Silver Lining Books, 2003.

Hawley, Casey Fitts. *Effective Letters for Every Occasion*. Barron's Educational Series, 2000.

Graber, Steven, and Barry Littmann. *Everything Online Job Search Book: Find the Jobs, Send Your Resume and Land the Career of Your Dreams—All Online!* Adams Media Corporation, 2000.

Greene, Susan D., and Melanie C. Martel. *The Ultimate Job Hunter's Guidebook*. Houghton Mifflin Company, 2000.

Ireland, Susan. *Complete Idiot's Guide to the Perfect Resume*. The Penguin Group, 2000.

Haldane's Best Cover Letters for Professionals. Impact Publications, 1999.

Holcombe, Marya. *The Best Letter Book Ever*. Round Lake Publishing, 2002.

Iacone, Salvatore J. *Write to the Point: How to Communicate with Style and Purpose*. Career Press, 2003.

Kennedy, Joyce Lain. *Cover Letters for Dummies*. John Wiley & Sons, 2000.

Krannich, Ronald L., and Caryl Rae Krannich. *Dynamite Cover Letters*. Impact Publications, 1999.

Krannich, Ronald L., and Caryl Rae Krannich. *The Savvy Resume Writer: The Behavioral Advantage*. Impact Publications, 1999.

Lamb, Sandra. *How to Write It: A Complete Guide to Everything You'll Ever Write*. Ten Speed Press, 1998.

McKinney, Anne, Editor. *Cover Letters That Blow Doors Open*. PREP Publishing, 1999.

McKinney, Anne, Editor. *Real Resumes for Career Changers: Actual Resumes and Cover Letters*. PREP Publishing, 2000.

McKinney, Anne, Editor. *Resumes and Cover Letters for Managers: Job-Winning Resumes and Letters for Management Positions*. PREP Publishing, 1999.

Merhish, Ferris E. *7,001 Resumes: The Job Search Workbook*. 1st Books Library, 2001.

Nichols, Harve L., and Walter L. Fortson. *Resume Writing Without Paid Work Experience*. Trafford Publishing, 2001.

Noble, David F. *Gallery of Best Cover Letters: A Collection of Quality Cover Letters by Professional Resume Writers*. JIST Works, Inc., 2000.

O'Neill, Lucy. *Job Smarts*. Scholastic Library Publishing, 2001.

Otfinoski, Steve. *Scholastic Guide to Putting It in Writing*. Scholastic, Inc., 1993.

Provenzano, Steve. *Blue Collar Resumes*. Career Press, 1999.

Resumes for First-Time Job Hunters. McGraw-Hill, 2000.

Rosenberg, Arthur, and David Hizer. *The Resume Handbook: How to Write Outstanding Resumes and Cover Letters for Every Situation*. Adams Media Corporation, 1996.

Troutman, Kathryn Kraemer, Brian Friel, and Mark Reichenbacher. *Electronic Federal Resume Guidebook*. The Resume Place, 2001.

Troutman, Kathryn Kraemer, and others. *Ten Steps to a Federal Job: Navigating the Federal Job System, Writing Federal Resumes and Cover Letters with a Mission*. The Resume Place, 2002.

Washington, Tom. *Resume Power: Selling Yourself on Paper in the New Millennium*. Mount Vernon Press, 2000.

Weber, Karl, and Rob Kaplan. *The Insider's Guide to Writing the Perfect Resume*. Peterson's, 2001.

Webster's New World Letter Writing Handbook. John Wiley & Sons, 2003.

Whitcomb, Susan Britton, and Pat Kendall. *e-Resumes: Everything You Need to Know About Using Electronic Resumes to Tap into Today's Hot Job Market*. McGraw-Hill, 2001.

Whitcomb, Susan Britton. *Resume Magic*. JIST Works, 2002.

Wynett, Stanley. *Cover Letters That Will Get You the Job You Want*. F & W Publications, 1993.

Yate, Martin John. *Resumes That Knock 'Em Dead!* Adams Media Corporation, 2000.

Appendix B
Selected Organizations of Interest

America's Career InfoNet
www.acinet.org

Canada Career Consortium
280 Albert St., Suite 903
Ottawa, Ontario, K1P 5G8
www.careerccc.org

ERI Economic Research Institute
8575 164th Ave. NE, Suite 100
Redmond, WA 98052
www.erieri.com

Job Accommodation Network
P.O. Box 6080
Morgantown, WV 26506-6080
www.jan.icdi.wvu.edu

National Association of Colleges and
Employers
62 Highland Ave.
Bethlehem, PA 18017-9085
www.jobweb.com

National Career Development Association
c/o Creative Management Alliance
10820 E. 45th St., Suite 210
Tulsa, OK 74146
www.ncda.org

Professional Association of Resume Writers
& Career Coaches
1388 Brightwaters Blvd. NE
St. Petersburg, FL 33704
www.parwcom

Public Library Association
www.pla.org

U.S. Equal Employment Opportunity
Commission
1801 L St. NW
Washington, DC 20507
www.eeoc.gov

Wider Opportunities for Women
1001 Connecticut Ave. NW, Suite 930
Washington, DC 20036
www.WOWonline.org

Women Work!
The National Network for Women's
Employment
1625 K St. NW, Suite 300
Washington, DC 20006
www.womenwork.org

Appendix C
Action Words

When writing cover letters, try to use as many action words (verbs) as you can. Action words liven up your cover letters and make them more interesting and readable to employers. Following are typical action words that you may wish to use in your cover letters.

accelerate	audit
accomplish	beautify
account	budget
achieve	build
act	buy
adapt	calculate
adjust	carve
administer	catalog
advertise	chart
advise	check
advocate	classify
alter	clean
analyze	coach
appraise	collate
approve	collect
arbitrate	command
arrange	communicate
assemble	compare
assign	complete
assist	compose

compound
compute
conceptualize
conduct
confront
conserve
construct
consult
contact
contribute
control
convert
cook
cooperate
coordinate
copy
correspond
counsel
count
create
critique
defend
delegate
deliver
demonstrate
design
detect
determine
develop
devise
diagnose
direct
discover
dispense
display
distribute
divert
double
draft
dramatize
draw
drive
edit

eliminate
encourage
enforce
enter
entertain
establish
estimate
evaluate
examine
exchange
execute
exercise
exhibit
expand
experiment
explain
express
facilitate
feed
file
find
fix
follow
forecast
formulate
gain
gather
generate
give
guard
guide
handle
harvest
heal
help
identify
imagine
implement
improve
increase
influence
initiate
innovate

inspect	perform
inspire	persuade
install	plan
instruct	plant
interpret	plaster
interview	play
introduce	polish
invent	pose
investigate	post
judge	preach
landscape	prepare
launch	prescribe
lay	present
lead	preside
learn	prevent
lift	print
listen	process
loan	produce
locate	program
mail	project
maintain	promote
manage	propose
measure	protect
mediate	provide
meet	pump
memorize	purchase
mentor	question
merchandise	quote
message	raise
model	read
modify	realize
monitor	receive
motivate	recognize
move	recommend
negotiate	record
obtain	recruit
operate	redesign
order	reduce
organize	refer
pack	register
package	rehabilitate
paint	relieve
patrol	remember

remove	style
render	succeed
reorganize	suggest
repair	summarize
repeat	supercede
replace	supervise
report	supply
represent	support
research	survey
restore	swim
review	synthesize
revise	tailor
revitalize	talk
ride	teach
route	tend
run	terminate
save	test
schedule	time
sculpt	tint
seat	tolerate
select	trace
sell	track
send	trade
serve	train
service	transfer
sew	transcribe
shampoo	treat
shape	trim
shave	triple
simplify	tune
sing	turn
sketch	tutor
solve	type
sort	usher
speak	verify
start	visualize
streamline	wash
strengthen	weigh
stress	welcome
stretch	widen
structure	win
study	wrap